Workshift

Future-Proof Your Organization for the 21st Century

Jason Morwick, Robyn Bews, Emily Klein, and Tim Lorman

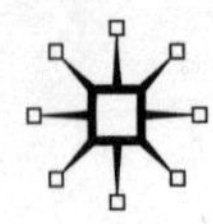

First published in 2013 by
PALGRAVE MACMILLAN®
in the United States—a division of St. Martin's Press LLC,
175 Fifth Avenue, New York, NY 10010.

Where this book is distributed in the UK, Europe and the rest of the world, this is by Palgrave Macmillan, a division of Macmillan Publishers Limited, registered in England, company number 785998, of Houndmills, Basingstoke, Hampshire RG21 6XS.

Palgrave Macmillan is the global academic imprint of the above companies and has companies and representatives throughout the world.

Palgrave® and Macmillan® are registered trademarks in the United States, the United Kingdom, Europe and other countries.

ISBN: 978–1–137–33746–7

Library of Congress Cataloging-in-Publication Data

Morwick, Jason M., 1972–
Workshift : future-proof your organization for the 21st century / Jason Morwick, Robyn Bews, Emily Klein, and Tim Lorman.
pages cm
ISBN 978–1–137–33746–7 (alk. paper)
1. Telecommuting. 2. Information technology—Management. 3. Corporate culture. I. Title.

HD2336.3.M67 2013
658.3′123—dc23 2013023101

A catalogue record of the book is available from the British Library.

Design by Newgen Knowledge Works (P) Ltd., Chennai, India.

First edition: December 2013

10 9 8 7 6 5 4 3 2 1

Printed in the United States of America.

Contents

Figures and Tables

Figures

Tables

Acknowledgments

Two years ago we had an audacious idea to write a book—audacious because we were four authors who didn't know each other and lived in two countries in four quadrants of North America. It is through the efforts of our project that we have come to believe, more than ever, in the value and future of virtual collaboration.

All virtual teams thrive on collaboration. Our team, spread between Boston, Calgary, Denver, and Orlando, was no exception. This book is the end product of the virtual relationships, collective effort, and shared knowledge between the authors and the many people who contributed their experiences. It would not have been possible without insight, encouragement, and feedback of our entire virtual team that included family, friends, colleagues, business leaders, and editors. We are especially grateful to our families—our "core team"—for their endless support that gave us the motivation, and for putting up with us, as we completed this endeavor.

Robyn

I would like to express my deepest appreciation to the team at Calgary Economic Development that has had the foresight to understand that while we don't always know where the path is going, it's an important one for us to be on. It's rare to find an employer who is really a partner.

To my husband Rich who continues to be my biggest supporter and advocate for my professional development, I thank you and love you. To the WHAT! Team for reminding me to have fun, thank you. I dedicate this book especially to Lucas and Felix (the shoemaker's children in many ways!); I am motivated by this life's work so that other moms and dads get to spend as much time enjoying their children as I do you. Love you "too much!" (And thank you for being quiet during conference calls.) And finally, thank you to my hometown Calgary for showing leadership and bravery in the new world of work!

Emily

A friend gave me advice not long ago, stating that you never end up where you originally planned when it comes to big undertakings—that the evolution of ideas have a way of taking on a life of their own, altering your course in surprising ways. Originally this book idea was birthed in pairs, and upon introduction to one another, we recognized our complementary strengths and unique benefits of joining forces. With a shared commitment to helping organizations chart a way forward, we are each passionate about realizing more future-focused workplaces. Professionally, my desire to see flexible workplaces take root and grow started decades ago and continues to drive what I believe is the most productive, and innovative way to work today.

Many thanks go to my husband Mike and daughter Kate for their ongoing support, love, and patience. A big thank you also to a great cadre of friends and colleagues, all of whom helped and inspired us with this book. Many of these colleagues, past and present, are those with whom I've shared a unique camaraderie, multiple virtual collaboration successes, and deep respect for the tenet that the whole is greater than the sum of its parts.

I hope we look back on this time as a pivotal turning point toward knowing rewarding careers are ones augmented by the people, communities, and companies that embrace the value of Workshift.

Tim

I wrote most of my portion of this book while sitting at the back table (the closest seat to the power outlet, coffee, and bathroom) of the Einstein's Bagel Shop in Highlands Ranch, Colorado. For weeks, I sat there transcribing notes, writing drafts, and participating in conference calls with my coauthors. During that time, Zack, Caleb, and the rest of the Einstein's team carefully prepared my complicated bagel order, mysteriously kept the seasonal "Winter Blend" coffee flavour on tap deep into April, flawlessly maintained the wireless signal, and mercifully held the myriad of things I would inevitably leave behind each day safe in the office until my next visit (also known as "tomorrow"). They taught me that it really does feel good to go to a place were everybody knows your name.

I would like to thank my wife Lisa for providing invaluable support and encouragement through the process of writing this book—I love you, buddy. I would also like to thank my kids: Every afternoon my son Charlie would check in on how my book was coming along, and my daughter Sydney would ask how many bagels I made that day (she was a little unclear on exactly what the whole "I'm going to work at the bagel shop" really meant).

Finally, I would like to thank Dave Glasscock for his mentorship (then and now). With his guidance and support, I have been able to successfully turn my profession into my passion.

Jason

Writing a book requires time away from other activities, such as spending time with those closest to you. As always, I am indebted to my wife Christa and children Ainslee and Maston. Their patience, support, and love continue to be my greatest source of motivation. I am grateful for their backing as I took on this project.

Workshift is a collection of stories, case studies, and anecdotes.

I also would like to thank my friends and colleagues for their many contributions to this book. It would not have been possible without their collaboration and insight.

We strongly believe that this book can help change organizations, and our communities, for the better. We do so hope you enjoy the very real stories about the transformation the organizations and individuals featured in this book have undergone in both their personal and professional lives by having the courage to adopt a culture of flexible work.

We also owe thanks to a strong network of colleagues and friends that helped us in many different ways—too numerous to name, we hope you know our gratitude is infinite.

Our virtual team would not be complete without our agent Jill Kramer from Waterside Productions, and our editors at Palgrave Macmillan, Laurie Harting and Lauren LoPinto. Jill enthusiastically embraced this project from the beginning and ensured it would find the proper home. We are thankful for Laurie and Lauren who guided us through the process and were always on hand to provide valuable feedback. Writing a book is not an easy task, and we were lucky to have Jill, Laurie, and Lauren to partner with us to ensure our idea would make it to print.

Thank you.

Introduction: The Evolved Workplace

> The world as we have created it is a process of our thinking. It cannot be changed without changing our thinking.
>
> —Albert Einstein

Not long ago, a corporate space and facility manager from a financial services firm was touring an office building with one of the company's investment asset managers. The space was purchased as an investment and would be leased to office tenants. It was a great investment—close to 50 thousand square feet of prime office space situated in the growing stretch between Los Angeles and San Diego.

There was only one small problem. The space was completely vacant. No workers bustling about. No symphony of clicking keyboards or drumming of copying machines. The air was absent of the coffee aroma from a nearby break room. No colorful pushpins stuck to the slate gray fabric of cubicle walls. Nothing but fluorescent lights and a bland carpet in need of cleaning. It was empty and quiet. What made it worse was that they both knew the building had been unoccupied for quite some time.

"You know, this is all your fault," the asset manager finally said, breaking the silence. The facility manager, leader of the company's work-from-home program, just stared back at the asset manager as he continued. "If it wasn't for you and all your 'just work from home and give back your office' noise, we wouldn't be in this mess of trying to lease all of this empty space."

Later, the facility manager sat alone in a coffee shop located between his home and office, thinking about what the asset manager had said. The café was full, but no one was just sitting and drinking coffee. Across from him, two men in formal business attire chatted away. From the way the younger man clutched a portfolio and crisply bound booklet of papers, it was clear he was in the middle of a job interview. Next to them, a casually dressed man with a thick briefcase sat across from an older couple reviewing a large stack of documents. On the other side of the café, four people engaged in a lively debate, gesturing wildly across the laptops in front of them. One of the members of the group pulled out a dry erase marker, turned, and began to write notes on the window of the store as if it was a whiteboard in a conference room. Other patrons tapped away on their tablets or talked into cell phones.

Technology and the way we live have changed radically and permanently. Our lives, the way we connect, communicate, and collaborate, have been so profoundly altered by technology that was so rapidly introduced we may forget how things were done just a few years ago. One doesn't have to look far to notice the social and economic trends that have already changed the way we interact: the consumerization of information technology (IT), the explosion of mobile technology, increased urbanization, climbing fuel prices, the repatriation of women to the workforce, generational shifts, and shrinking office space per employee to name a few.

"Work" used to be a place where you went during the day, and now it's something that can be done anywhere. Sheldon Dyck, president of ATB Investor Services, one of the many companies we profile in this book, observed: For centuries work happened largely one way and we entrenched a lot of habits about how work happens. The industrial revolution required people to be around an assembly line to produce something, so did the manufacturing era where you had to be in one place to work with other people and produce a car or whatever you were making. Then we entered the information age where more of us began contributing ideas versus doing physical labor, but you still had to be in the building to access the computers that were joined together with wires that could only reach so far, so we created skyscrapers to house everyone. We had centuries of a reality where in order to do work we had to be physically close.

Organizational leaders still struggle with the notion that this version of work is the most efficient, even in this age of technology, mobility, and flexibility. While attending a business conference, we informally asked several conference participants if their employers had flexible work programs in place. All but a few responded "no."

"There's no way our executives would support it. They are against the idea of telework or telecommuting," one of them said as he walked away, thumbing through emails on his smart phone.

Bookshelves and conference agendas are full of books and presentations about changes in the workplace. For decades, people have preached about how we will work differently in the near future. *This is not a book about telecommuting*, a middle-aged term coined over 30 years ago. Telecommuting was born in the early 1970s, long before the dawn of cloud-based computing, VoIP, instant messaging, desktop sharing applications, telepresence, or ubiquitous use of email and mobile devices. Perhaps its failure to take hold in many organizations was because it was an idea ahead of its time. As technology evolved, telecommuting gave way to telework.

This is not a book about telework. Telework promised to lower operating costs, reduce an organization's carbon footprint, boost productivity, and create happier employees. The telework era, still an ongoing effort, was a great improvement over telecommuting. Unfortunately, telework has become synonymous with working from home, and employees have become divided into those that work in traditional office assignments and those that telework.

Beyond telework is the concept of mobile work that is replacing notions of telecommuting and teleworking altogether. There are an estimated 20–30 million teleworkers in the United States. However, when we try to capture numbers around teleworkers, traditional workers working from home after hours or working while they are traveling are often left out of the equation. Global market intelligence firm International Data Corporation estimates that there are already one billion mobile workers worldwide and by the end of 2013 a third of the workforce will be mobile. The explosion in mobility and more mobile workers is amplified by the growing use of personal mobile devices, including smart phones and tablets, and mobile applications.

In this book, we explore how the workplace of yesterday, if it remains the same, will soon become an expensive collection of vacant and underutilized space. We present case studies of how organizations have successfully embraced the strategy of evolving or adapting their workplaces in ways that align with how their employees work today, and how significant benefits have been realized for both the organizations and employees alike.

For example, we know the chief executive officer (CEO) of an Internet services company that grew increasingly concerned over reports of a well-known competitor that was gaining market share. It was rumored that current employees were being lured away to work for them. To rub salt in the wound, he was told that prospective employees were excited when they spoke about opportunities to interview with the competitor firm.

Was this other company offering more financial incentives to employees, or better salaries and bonuses, he asked himself. Were they being promised faster promotions, more exciting assignments? What would make employees leave? To obtain more information, the vice president (VP) of human resources (HR) was sent to an industry conference where her peer from the competitor company was presenting on a panel addressing innovations in workplace design.

"We have spent the entire past year rolling out a mobile work program for our employees that was the result of an in-depth assessment of how we needed to change our workplace practices to remain a competitive, exciting, and attractive place to work," she said. "In conjunction with this assessment, we surveyed our staff to find out what made them happy, why they decided to work for us, what made them stay and what would make them leave."

The company discovered that their employees wanted and needed more control over how they worked, both independently and collaboratively in teams. Employees were feeling an unyielding sense of information overload and were overwhelmed by an increasing workload that required staying later in the office. These experiences were burning out employees, leading some to consider other employment options.

"Our company had always issued new laptops for our employees and allowed employees the flexibility they needed to work core hours, come into work late or leave early as needed while making up for that time at a later point," the presenter shared. "We had a telecommuting policy but no established mobile work program.

We discovered our employees wanted to work in a different type of way. They wanted more opportunities to work remotely, as needed, or during off business hours when they travelled. They wanted our company to support this increasingly mobile work style with the right tools, technologies and training. It was important for them to feel they could easily collaborate with colleagues and other teams, in or out of the office, in a way that worked for them both personally and professionally."

The listening HR executive took in the information and knew it hit a nerve. They too issued laptops in their company, had similar tools and technology the other firm had, and offered some flexible work policies for their employees. But she heard several recent reports from employees complaining that managers were resistant to letting their direct reports work from home and that they were not fully supporting the need for flexible schedules.

> We took this information seriously and tried to figure how it would work for us from a business perspective. How do we let our employees loose like this globally and still have control over the ability to exceed expectations of our clients and meet our financial goals? What would this cost us from setting up our employees in remote offices and managing them that way? What Return on Investment (ROI) would the company achieve? Allowing employees this kind of freedom to work differently seemed, at times, unrealistic. In other ways, it made complete sense. A more mobile work environment was what early career employees were asking for. Seasoned employees were also asking for more flexibility to address the need for greater work-life integration. After the mobile work program was rolled out, we held information sessions and surveys with employees to solicit candid feedback. The results were overwhelmingly positive. Employees were extremely pleased that the company had listened to them and engaged them in creating a mobile work program that worked. We are now considered a Best Place to Work in our region.

The VP of HR had quite a bit to report back to the senior leadership team and the CEO. Corporate executives never considered rolling out a program in a more formalized way and thought they were doing enough in offering an informal policy, one that was perceived as an employee perk. With all of this new information, she knew a burning question would be what they should do with it.

From Changes in Our Personal to Professional Lives

In the past, changes to the way we work drove changes to the way we lived. During the Industrial Revolution, the use of electricity as a tool was first realized in the factory, not the home. Early computers were used for business, not personal use, and the first email systems were used to enable scientists and researchers to communicate with each other. Now the paradigm is reversed. A unique characteristic of our current era is that a significant portion of workers have evolved while the organizations they work for have not. Today, organizations are scrambling to adopt ways to leverage the innovations their employees use so fluently. Consider the following:

- Why are "old-school" desktop computers still prevalent in the office to do work while we use powerful and sophisticated mobile devices that we take with us everywhere to manage our personal lives?
- When we have a problem or question in our personal life, why do we reach out to vast amounts of people simultaneously via social networks but still rely on a handful of specific individuals or chain of commands at work?
- Why does a manager need to see an employee in order to manage them, yet we maintain relationships with people we hardly meet in person using streaming video, instant messaging, file sharing, and collaboration networks?
- Why is email still a primary mode of communication at work when we easily use a variety of communication tools, whether it is Facebook, Twitter, and Skype to communicate with friends?
- Why do organizations cite security as a barrier to allowing employees to work outside the office, yet the same employees can use consumer applications for banking or other personal activities from any location?

For the first time, mobile devices and networks, both computer and social, are more sophisticated and pervasive for employees outside of work than at work. The next revolution in the workplace, one that is now underway, is being driven not by business but by its employees. We call this revolution Workshift.

The Shift to a New Way to Work

In its simplest form, *Workshift is about working where and when we are most effective.* Workshift is about accepting change and overcoming resistance. Resistance that is so profound, even when the change has occurred and has been embedded into almost every facet of our lives we still believe we can negotiate it, resist it, or try to "manage" it. Perhaps this explains why so many organizations struggle with implementing traditional telework or telecommuting programs. Recent research all point to people, not technology, as the main barrier. A Booz Allen Hamilton and Partnership for Public Service study revealed that managers were the largest single factor among barriers to telework adoption.[1] In the same year, a Mineta Transportation Institute study also found that the most significant resistance to telecommuting comes from lack of senior management support and organizational culture.[2] The challenges one US Federal agency faced highlights this resistance.

A chief of program analysis and evaluation (PA&E) we know reflected on how his organization began the transformation to comply with the Telework Enhancement Act (TEA) of 2010, legislation that granted US Federal employees eligibility to telework and required Federal agencies to establish telework policies. It was the end of the day, he was ready to go home, but did not look forward to the usual 90-minute commute that often confronted him as he traversed the DC streets to get to the Beltway. The commute and traffic patterns had gotten noticeably worse during his tenure at this Federal government agency, and he often thought about the impact stressful long commutes had on him, his personal life, and his health.

He was adept with technology and had worked closely with the IT division to help promote new technologies that had been deployed agency-wide to streamline business processes and build more collaborative work teams. Most of these new tools were well received, and employees were excited to migrate from using legacy systems known for creating data silos in applications that were not relational with other updated systems in the agency. It was an interesting year observing the behavior changes both in his staff and throughout other divisions as they began using collaborative tools, instant messaging software, and mobile devices. At times it seemed the winds of change fueling the new technology adoption sweeping his agency was a synchronistic collaborator with the effort to simultaneously pilot telework.

After an agency review of what types of positions could participate in telework, his division had been selected to participate in a pilot that was part of an agency-wide initiative to comply with TEA legislation and respond to the growing cacophony of employees seeing other agencies more readily allow their staff to telework. He was cautiously optimistic that a pilot could be successful, but was all too familiar with the ingrained culture his agency had and wasn't quite sure how long-time government managers would easily adapt to this new working environment. The pilot program came with policies and procedures for his division, along with a strategic communications program that highlighted the benefits of telework through webinars, and a plan to showcase success stories published on the agency's intranet. As the pilot began, several employees in his division submitted requests. A few employees requested telework agreements for one or two days a week, while others opted for full weeks. Each manager and employee was required to participate in a telework training module online prior to commencing an agreement.

The pilot took place over several months and was met with mixed reviews. The results from surveys indicated that some employees needed more support in teleworking because they were feeling disconnected despite the new technology and that their relationship with their managers had changed. Others felt liberated and happier that they were no longer tethered to their office space and commented that their reduction in commute times made life much less stressful for them. It wasn't hard to discern the real story behind the two different categories of employees, those who adapted more easily to telework and those who did not. It was reported that the managers who participated in telework days themselves were much more amenable to managing distributed work teams, trusted their employees more, and made concerted efforts to build and strengthen a team culture that embraced technology and new norms. Other reports indicated a tense atmosphere, with certain telework employees feeling unsupported by managers who on the one hand signed telework agreements, but did not participate themselves. These employees reported that their managers were suspicious of their activities, questioning whether they were performing their duties and tasks on telework days and generally made it difficult to communicate with them. In several instances these employees indicated that telework made them feel like their relationships within the agency were more uncertain and that they could potentially lose their jobs more easily than if they were in the office.

In the backdrop of this feedback, the chief of PA&E understood that telework was here to stay, but the agency had taken a more basic approach to implementation, exposing myriad issues in the organizational culture. Without addressing how to make this shift culturally, he was uncertain the needs of employees who wanted to telework would be met as they rolled out the program agency-wide. Figuring out how to take the next steps seemed like going from one end of a maze to another.

The chief of PA&E is not alone in his experience. Significant variability exists in the amount of resistance companies have in embracing acceptance of a new culture within their workplace. When pressed, organizational leaders question their ability to absorb the perceived change to the workplace, worry about the impact on corporate culture, argue about the cost to make the transition, and dispute the measurable benefits. All these arguments point to an assumption that workplace change is perceived as an "all-or-nothing" endeavor. We disagree. Our research shows there is significant variability in the way that organizations have accepted and successfully implemented a Workshift culture. We will highlight the many shades of success and the different pathways to get there.

In This Book

This book is both an instructive guide to realizing Workshift in any organization and a collection of best practices from several companies across the public and private sectors that have adopted this new culture. The consistent themes from these organizations include:

- How each transformed their culture as a component of their overall business strategy (it wasn't an "all-or-nothing" proposition).
- How none of the programs began as large or as sophisticated as they are today; they all followed an incremental path of crawl-walk-run strategy.

- How some organizations realized they were evolving rather than reinventing their organizational culture. Many found they were simply consolidating and formalizing the myriad of informal flexible work arrangements, agreements, and processes that were already being used.
- How disruptive workplace trends impacted each organization: the profound impact mobile tools and technologies have had in how and when employees worked, and the need to reduce corporate real estate (CRE) and redesign office space to fit a more collaborative way of working that fosters innovation and supports mobility.

Why I left an organization that didn't have flexible work

Leah Sobering, Workopolis

Leah Sobering, a top performing account manager from *Workopolis* tells us her story. (Workopolis is a Canadian company offering online career solutions: allowing employers to post jobs and candidates to post resumes in order to connect online. The company also offers career management tools and advice.) Leah's story highlights the changing expectations of employees in the modern workplace and how organizations need to adapt to win the war in talent.

"I had been with Workopolis for three years, based remotely in Calgary and enjoying the flexibility of a home office. As an action-orientated person I quickly adapted to life outside of an office as this meant I could work whenever and wherever I wanted, so long as I was achieving my goals and targets. And I did regularly overachieve in part due to the flexibility I had to work how I wanted—including when and where. If Tuesday at 2 p.m. wasn't a peak productivity time for me I could step away and engage in something non-work related, always then coming "back to work" to finish what I set out to accomplish, usually refreshed and reenergized. Work/life balance was no longer a "balance" per se, rather a fusion and that works for me 100 percent.

After three years I briefly left Workopolis for another company and a new opportunity, and while the new Employer and myself had the best intentions of a great fit, it didn't prove to be a success for either one of us. The organization did not embrace a flexible work environment, at least not to the extent I had grown so accustomed, and I quickly realized I was not able to adapt to their corporate culture. In some ways it was unfortunate, as I really pride myself on being a successful employee in any organization I've belonged; I've enjoyed lateral and promotional moves with all past Employers (most of whom had some form of flexibility within their organization). Ultimately it was ideal for me to have this experience as it gave me perspective and reinforced at the core I am a Workshifter.

After a brief 5 months away I returned to Workopolis in a new and exciting role."

With each case study, we examine several factors that we have identified as being critical for designing and implementing a successful program, specifically:

- How was senior leadership involved in championing the program?
- How was senior management engaged in creating, accepting, and implementing the program?
- What were the strategic objectives of the program and were they clearly communicated?
- How was program success measured?
- How were program participants selected?
- What was the program's impact on the CRE portfolio?
- What was the financial impact of the program?
- How did the program maintain connectivity between employees and managers?
- What resources were needed to get started and what resources were required to scale the program?
- What kind of training was delivered to managers and employees?
- What steps did the program follow from inception to implementation?

Our objective is to provide readers with a broader understanding and a vocabulary of terms and processes to facilitate comparison between programs implemented with different goals across a spectrum of work environments. This understanding can then be used to aid in the strategic planning, program design, and implementation process for other organizations.

This book is designed to serve as a handbook for HR, CRE, IT executives, and organizational leaders. We will show how organizations have accepted and fully embraced the seismic shifts in how, when, and where we work. Case studies, checklists, and knowledge centers will provide the information and resources necessary to enable organizational leaders to understand and accept the evolved work culture of their employees, and to design a program that leverages advantages and minimizes challenges of accepting the way we now work.

To help you, we've developed a blueprint and methodology to lead you to a new way of working. Before you start your journey, chapter 1, The Workshift Spectrum, will illustrate that there is no single formula to describe an organization's transformation. We will highlight the many approaches and how to identify where your organization lies on the spectrum. Each subsequent chapter will take you step-by-step through the various stages of development.

We wrap up the book with a look at potential trends and how these trends will continue to shape the future work environment, leaders, and employees. Work will continually change as new technology evolves, people's attitudes and desires change, demographics shift, infrastructure adjusts, and new legislation is passed. Finally, we offer some advice for leaders on what they can do to prepare themselves and their organizations to be successful in the continued workplace evolution. We'll also conclude by highlighting the potential changes we're likely to see, not just in organizations, but in our communities as well.

As you will learn, Workshift is a model that has been tested in both private- and public-sector entities. It has been deployed in organizations with only a handful of employees and large multinational conglomerates. Most interestingly, however, it has been vetted in boom and bust economies. It is effective at providing a solution to reducing unnecessary CRE expenses, leveraging technology that renders employees location independent, and increasing flexibility to support a work environment that is effective, sustainable, healthy, and meets evolving business goals.

CHAPTER 1

The Workshift Spectrum

We can chart our future clearly and wisely only when we know the path which has led to the present.

—Adlai E. Stevenson

Although we typically refer to Workshift as a program or initiative, it does not represent a single workplace approach, program, or strategy. It is a collection of methods that organizations use to align employee work styles and manage goals with business needs. The intended result of this improved alignment is a more efficient work environment that provides employees and their organizations with numerous benefits.

We refer to Workshift as a spectrum. While everyone may have the same expectations for realizing benefits, businesses, organizations, and people tackle similar issues in radically different ways. We believe this phenomenon is the key challenge with adoption. Until now, no one has developed a comprehensive road map supporting adoption by entities and people across varying sectors in dissimilar stages of workplace strategy maturity.

However, recognizing differences is not enough. We know that organizations want to find out "who else is doing it?" and "when are we going to get there?" before embarking on change. They want the comfort of feeling that they are not blazing a trail alone and that they will know when they arrive at their destination. We believe leadership accepts the inevitability of change in our workplaces; however, they simultaneously wish to avoid risks associated with either trailblazing or being left behind. For alternative workplace arrangements, this has meant a decade of awkward implementation steps and stagnation occurring at the same time.

Workshift: The ability to work where and when employees and managers determine they are the most effective or needed, and in a work environment where employees and managers are supported by the organization's leadership, IT infrastructure, and culture.

For some, the shift is all about framing. Positioning Workshift as a drastic change in the way business is done is a mistake. We have often caught ourselves waxing about "the future of work" and other such zealous terminology. Recently, a professor who has done extensive research on telework pulled us aside and said, "Stop scaring the sh** out of people! You need to remind them that we are already working differently and in many cases this is not a huge change at all!" On this point, one client we worked with presented his organization's leadership with a comprehensive plan for adoption of a telework model. It was rejected on the basis that "telework" (the word our client had elected to use in the proposal) was too radical. Our client did a search and replace on the document, changing all references to "telework" with "Workshift" and resubmitted the proposal several months later. His leadership team accepted the document and felt it was a more realistic proposal than the previous one. Why? Because our client took the time to communicate the evolution of work today in a way that was better understood by his leadership team. Ideas, norms, and work practices become so embedded in organizational cultures that any new idea that appears to run counter to established beliefs is often rejected before it is evaluated or considered. Often, it is only a matter of how new ideas are presented or introduced. This book also discusses the psychology of framing and positioning these programs, and why this is a critical component of your plan.

In today's vernacular, many terms used to describe the modern workplace are used synonymously or overlap at the very least. Workshift is the umbrella term that helps describe all of these growing work practices. Here are a few common terms used by many organizations today:

- *Flextime/flexwork*: Working a full- or part-time schedule, but adjusting start and end times to accommodate personal needs or commitments, which allows employees more choices in managing their work schedule.
- *Telework*: Working a full- or part-time schedule from a location other than an employer's designated workplace. Telework includes working from a home site office, co-working/telework center, or anywhere else that is outside a traditional corporate or government office.
- *Telecommuting*: Often used synonymously with the word "telework." Historically, telecommuting was defined as using technology to work from anywhere to reduce commuting time. In many organizations, telecommuting refers to part-time work from home, while telework refers to full-time work-from-home status.
- *Remote working*: Working in a location where the employee has no physical interaction with customers/clients or other employees. Usually refers to arrangements where employees have no access to an employer's workplace.
- *Workplace flexibility*: Defines how, when, and where work gets done that is mutually synergistic for both employers and employees. It is a commitment from employers to build a more flexible organizational culture to meet employee needs for work-life integration (in a more seamless way).
- *Mobility*: The ability of employees, with appropriate tools, technology, and flexible workplace policies, to perform work either inside or outside an organization in a way that accommodates multiple modes of working.
- *Distributed work teams (aka virtual teams)*: Teams in which at least one team member is not geographically located with the rest of the team. Teams may work together permanently or on a temporary basis and may cut across organizational/functional groups.

Throughout this book we describe an approach that will make your experience feel customized, while you simultaneously read stories of other companies that have faced similar challenges.

Through research we have learned that there is no single formula to describe an organization's transformation to a new work culture. Some changes are driven from the top-down, motivated by executive leaders needing to immediately reduce operating costs, change their business model to become more competitive, or, for some public-sector organizations, comply with legal mandates. Other organizations change from bottom-up, resulting from a grassroots push from employees to increase work-life balance and job satisfaction. There are also organizations that fall somewhere in between, where mid-level leaders innovate and adapt to meet the rapidly changing technology devices that are invading the workplace or tools used in the personal lives of employees that also promise to impact business processes in ways never seen before. We highlight the many approaches and how to identify where your organization lies on the spectrum.

Our objective is to help you navigate your way through this turbulent sea of mega-change in the work environment. We recognize that depending on where you and your organization are in this spectrum of evolution, the support, tools, and resources you need are greatly varied. We believe that the methodology and principles remain the same, regardless of the industry, sector, or size of the organization. However, the specific tactics or details may be tailored or customized to fit the organization based on its progress. This book is designed in a similar fashion. Some readers will only need to skim the pages of the early chapters, confirming the steps necessary for creating a new organizational culture, ones that may be tested and known. Others will want to focus on the first portion of the book in order to establish their program and set their company up for success. We believe that anyone starting a program or managing one in progress can benefit from all the information and case studies presented, but need not feel the need to read it from cover to cover like a traditional business book. Like all parts of your business, your needs are unique. (But it's always good to test your assumptions!)

Throughout the book we identify sections, case studies, and anecdotes through a series of visual cues that are particularly important to an organization's approach to driving adoption. This will help you focus on the elements most critical to you at your particular juncture.

Common Organizational Approaches

As a starting point, you should first identify your organization's approach. This approach will impact how quickly the program is adopted and determine the specific tactics needed to ensure a successful implementation. Two key questions can help determine an organization's current approach. First, who wants the change? Is the push coming from the upper echelons of the organization or is it coming from the middle or lower levels? Second, has the organization attempted some form of telework or flexible work arrangements in the past? Is there an ad hoc approach to telework or flexible work that is up to a manager's discretion? Or, are there existing telecommuting, telework, or flexible work policies in place, even if no one is utilizing them? Has the organization formally launched a program and made some progress, only to hit a wall and stop progressing? Based on the answers to these questions, we have found through our research five basic approaches to assess the current state of your organization:

1. *Top-down*: In many cases, this common approach results from a significant business issue, such as a pending real estate transaction that requires tough decisions to be made by the most senior executives. For example, a friend of ours working for a large technology company called us one day in a panic. Her company was expanding and senior leaders realized that they would have to add more office space to accommodate the increase in headcount.

   "I just received an email from the department head stating that by next week we have to clear out our cubicles because we all have to start working from home," she frantically said. With little guidance, expectations, or training, employees were simply expected to adhere to the new policy in order to help reduce the company's real estate footprint.

   "Do you think I can take my chair home with me? I don't have an ergonomically built chair at home and need one badly," she asked. We thought she was joking, but the sad reality was that employees had many unanswered questions and little time to prepare.

Top-down approaches are often characterized by their swift and decisive speed, very senior executive support, and their lack of HR considerations. Team members are left scratching their heads when they are transitioned into these new work arrangements and managers may be ill equipped to manage their new remote teams. At the extreme, this approach can also be known as "Workshift by brute force" when senior management mandates the change on the organization.

We are not suggesting, however, that all top-down methods are negative. In some cases, a top-down approach can be very effective if enough consideration is given to how the change will impact workers. As we discuss in later chapters, a condition for long-term *successful* implementations require executive sponsorship and commitment in creating a more flexible work culture. From the top, senior leaders play an important role in embracing and communicating the vision for realizing that change, and must build alignment among other executive leaders within the organization, helping them to understand the strategic business value and ROI of a creating a culture that supports the virtual workplace.

Starting in 2011, US federal agencies were required to comply with the TEA and develop policies to support telework. Many agency executives were quick to adopt the new legislation and enforce the new policies through all levels of their organization. An organization may adopt a top-down approach for a variety of reasons, not just to comply with legislative mandates or to quickly reduce its real estate costs. Some organizations may suffer talent shortages and be forced to attract talent outside their geographic area. Other organizations may have to react quickly to retain employees by offering them greater work-life integration or flexible work schedules, or risk losing talent to competitors. Regardless of the reason, senior leaders may have to move quickly and choose to push change from the top. We highlight a few of these success stories throughout this book from public and private sectors that demonstrate how leaders drove successful telework implementations by providing senior-level sponsorship, socializing the concept, conducting training and pilots, establishing metrics, and continuously reviewing progress.

2. *Revitalize*: In some cases, old programs need a fresh start. Somewhere in the company cloud there may be an old telecommuting policy you can dust off from several years ago. When you inquire about it, your VP of HR may tell you a policy exists and may be able to name one or two employees who are enjoying the benefits because of extenuating circumstances, but she quietly suggests that it's probably not going to be a program you see enjoyed ubiquitously by the masses.

   Existing policies and practices can provide a great starting point. Interested leaders can gather information and take a deep dive into what's working and what's not. Surveys of employees participating in current flexible work, telecommuting, or telework programs can provide data on the benefits or barriers to future efforts. Are employees experiencing greater work-life balance and more satisfaction? Higher employee satisfaction can be correlated to greater retention and may begin to build the business case for expanding or building on existing policies. Conversely, it's equally important to understand the challenges employees are facing. Do they have the right equipment and technical support? Is management supportive, or do employees fear that management will hold it against them if they are not in a designated office space every day? Knowing the hurdles that need to be overcome can help leaders develop a plan that specifically targets problem areas and ultimately increases adoption.
3. *Off-track*: Sometimes a program can't be revitalized because it's off track and needs a complete overhaul. This is not an approach anyone takes by choice, and a series of remediation actions to correct a program gone bad is often necessary. For example, a supply chain company we know conducted an annual employee satisfaction survey and discovered that overall employee morale was low and many talented employees intended to seek employment elsewhere. One of the chief complaints was poor work-life balance. As a result, the HR team developed a telecommuting policy to allow employees greater flexibility. The policy was signed off and supported by the president of the company who personally communicated his excitement of the new flexible work option. A pilot was conducted and the participants reported an increase in their

job satisfaction. A program manager from HR was assigned to develop and monitor metrics of success as the program was rolled out to the rest of the organization. After six months, the program fizzled. No one was telecommuting, not even those who participated in the pilot. The program manager and the rest of the HR team were left wondering why they became derailed.

This scenario is common for many organizations. The program starts out with early indicators of success—right level of sponsorship, clearly defined policies and expectations, success metrics, and perhaps a successful pilot. However, for a few reasons, it never gets off the ground. The organizational culture may not support the policies, or management resistance pressures employees not to change their work habits because these managers feel threatened by a loss of control or cannot understand how to foster and sustain high-performing virtual teams. In these cases, it is often hard to evolve ingrained perceptions about workplace productivity beyond traditional notions of passive face time. Whatever the reasons, a program in this milieu needs immediate triage to move forward.

4. *Grassroots*: Far from a top-down approach is the grassroots approach. Small pockets of this may be happening in the company, perhaps in certain divisions where employees are apt to work remotely from one to five days a week. In these instances, you may not be sure if your organization has a formal policy in place, but some forward-thinking managers are managing their teams by encouraging flexible work. Alternatively, as employees become more mobile, they bring in their own mobile devices or personal practices into the workplace. This practice alone, a trend that will grow exponentially in years ahead, is pressuring organizations to think more flexibly about how, where, and when work is done by their employees. This often leads to greater receptivity to creating organizational cultures that support mobile workers. Sometimes programs are "skunk works" in nature, possessively embraced by the teams participating and quietly resented by those that aren't. One large global biotech firm we know experienced this cultural disconnect. The company went through an acquisition, and the acquiring company

had long allowed employees to adopt flexible work schedules while the acquired company had not. The fusion of work teams across both organizations that had now become one was fraught with obstacles, in large part because resistance and quiet resentment had come to characterize interactions between managers in how, when, and work was being done.

5. *Workshift au naturel*: At the opposite end of the spectrum is the au naturel approach. Some organizations evolve a work program informally or as an organic outcome of their growing business. This may be common with many start-ups or small businesses. When a business venture is launched with only a small number of employees, each member may be on the road soliciting new business or working long hours from home to get the business off the ground. Office space may be limited—employees either work in a shared space or are completely virtual owing to the cost of real estate. Distributed work teams may be a necessity if the organization taps into employees with needed skill sets that are outside the organization's geographic area, or perhaps employees are strategically located to be near potential customers. Employees may already leverage their own personal mobile devices, social networks, or collaborative applications to get work done. This description may even apply to more mature organizations. The commonality among organizations that follow this approach is that no formal telework or flexible work policies may exist, but employees are already mobile, working from home, or working together virtually.

As the organization grows, business and IT leaders may need to pause to consider formalizing their approach. Leaders can better optimize efficiencies, improve group dynamics, and minimize risks by instituting a more structured program. It's important to point out that creating a formal program does not mean that management is stifling innovation or limiting employees. The organization is proactively taking steps to mitigate potential problems that can include everything from security issues due to uncontrolled or unknown devices on the network, to the high costs of multiple overlapping platforms, or conflicts between employees and managers over nonstandard work practices.

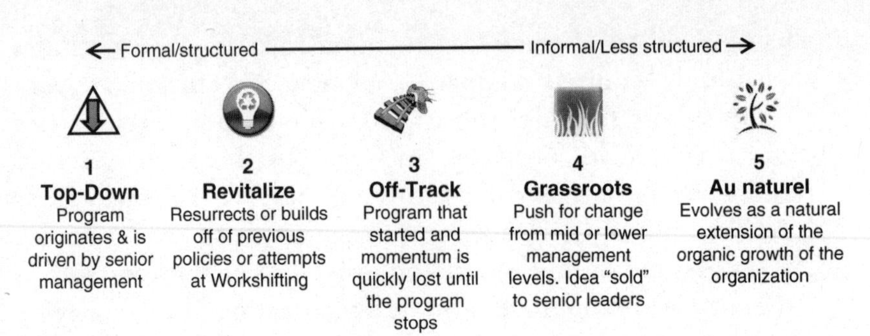

Figure 1.1 Workshift organization approach continuum.

We realize there are many variations of the scenarios above, but our collective experiences have demonstrated that general categorization can help your organization understand its starting point. To provide more clarity on the next steps to take, you should identify which stage of development your organization is in (summarized in figure 1.1).

Stages of Development

If your organization already has existing policies or has attempted this change in the past, you may already have completed the due diligence required to perform a gap analysis/assessment or create a business case. Other organizations may be starting from the beginning in a grassroots effort to create a new program from scratch. The seven stages below describe each phase of creating a program/culture from beginning to end, but not all the steps may be needed, given an organization's approach and what has been done in the past. Each phase has a series of activities, risks, and deliverables. The deliverables are decision points marking the end of each phase. Although some tasks can be done concurrently, we don't recommend moving into the next phase without successfully completing the deliverables from the previous phase. To help get you started, we have included a quick survey that will support an assessment of your status in flexible work adoption. This should be used only as a guiding tool—trust your instincts too! Quickly answer the questions below:

1. Has your organization developed a high-level business case or value proposition?
2. Is there a committed sponsor to champion the effort?

3. Is Workshift aligned to broader strategic goals?
4. Does leadership understand the current state (from an HR and IT perspective) and how far it is from the desired state?
5. Has the idea been socialized and does leadership support it?
6. Has a detailed implementation plan been developed?
7. Has a comprehensive communication and change management/acceptance plan been developed?
8. Has the program been launched (or a pilot initiated)?
9. Are success metrics tracked and reported to senior management?
10. Has Workshift met its intended ROI?
11. Is the organization prepared to expand the initiative to others areas?

If you answered no to all the questions above, your organization is in the earliest phase of development, Investigate. If you could answer yes only to the first two questions, your organization is in the Discover stage. Answering yes to the first five questions indicates you are in the Design stage. Affirmative answers to questions one through six indicate the organization is in the next stage, Engage. Yes to questions one through seven, Launch stage. Yes to questions one through eight, Measure stage. Finally, if you can answer yes to all the questions above, the organization is in the last stage of development, Leverage.

1. *Investigate*: You or others in your organization may be notionally interested in the concept, but would like to understand more about the benefits. You may have had a senior manager ask you to "look into telework" or you may be hearing about other organizations adopting programs to reduce real estate and attract or keep employees. Executives in your organization may be looking for ways to reduce costs or improve employee retention. You or other interested parties may want to know if this is something you should even consider for your team, department, or entire organization.

Like any large initiative, leaders define their vision before jumping into action. We've found that successful organizations start by defining the assumptions, scope, business drivers, and metrics of success. The high-level business case has to be agreed upon before it can cascade through the organization. Regardless of the size of the organization, industry, or public or private sector, a coherent strategy needs to be developed and demonstrably linked to larger strategic goals of an organization for it to be most successful.

Some of the key activities in this phase are:

- Research
- Finding case studies within the community/industry
- Creating the elevator pitch, answering the question "why would you do this?"
- Socializing the concept internally, formally or informally

Deliverables for the Investigate stage are:

- High-level business case (that demonstrates the ROI value for implementation)
- Committed sponsor or champion willing to take the idea forward

Some of the key risks of this phase are:

- Not finding enough credible information fast enough to build your case
- Not identifying a sponsor or champion within executive ranks
- Not getting enough airplay to communicate the concept

2. *Discover*: Strategy is an organization's compass, but leaders need a map. There is an important pre-step before creating the map, or operational plan. Leaders need to identify their starting point. Many organizations go through a discovery phase to gather data, test assumptions, and identify gaps and opportunities. From an organization and technology perspective, the ability to discern organization readiness and how far the organization stands from the desired end state is an important step in the discovery process.

Some of the key activities in this phase are:

- Gathering data
- Clearly defining the end state

- Identifying and validating assumptions
- Performing gap analysis (IT and organization)

Deliverables for the Discover stage are:

- Demonstration of how Workshift links to broader strategic goals
- Completed gap analysis
- Clearly defined business case

Some of the key risks of this phase are:

- Not collecting organizational data in a timely manner
- Conflicting management views on the end state
- Difficult to get an audience with key decision-makers

3. *Design*: Using information gathered in the Discover phase, leaders can now create a detailed operational plan for deployment. The elements of this plan should include a communications strategy, technology strategy, pilot strategy, and risk mitigation strategy. We provide examples and different approaches of how several organizations designed their initiatives and what successes and challenges they encountered along the way.

Some of the key activities in this phase are:

- Census building and leadership alignment—understanding why the organization is doing this and the key outcomes the organization cares about
- Developing a program charter, including key outcomes, deliverables, measurements, and scope
- Communication planning
- Determining training requirements
- Selecting the program team including project sponsor (needs to be as high up the food chain as you can go!)

Deliverables for the Design stage are:

- Program charter
- Identified, committed program resources
- Success metrics

Some of the key risks of this phase are:

- Pockets of influential resistance
- Program team does not have time allocated to focus on the initiative
- Limited time focused on planning

4. *Engage*: Plans are only as good as the people who are carrying them out. Leaders need to engage other organizational leaders at all levels, to socialize ideas, solicit feedback, and gain buy-in. Empirical research over recent years has consistently shown that management resistance is the number one barrier to telework or flexible work programs. Successful organizations address root causes of management resistance and what they did to turn detractors into advocates.

Some of the key activities in this phase are:

- Census building and communication
- Addressing existing limitations of organizational culture and management behavior that may inhibit adoption
- Storytelling—why this is great for the company, employees, and community
- Myth-busting

Deliverables for the Engage stage are:

- Communication plan
- Stakeholder analysis
- Change acceptance plan
- Success stories or case studies

Some of the key risks of this phase are:

- Nobody signs up (this is a symptom of something besides desire)
- Certain managers block participation, knowingly and/or unknowingly
- Senior leaders are not giving enough attention or airtime to the program

5. *Launch*: With a clear strategy, an understanding of an organization's current capabilities, a detailed plan, and management support, leaders are ready to implement. Now it's time

to execute. You may have a pilot team that has already been working from home. You may even receive positive feedback on the program, but like anything, there are bumps in the road. During this phase a focus on ongoing communication, manager and employee training, and pilot execution are critically important.

Some of the key activities in this phase are:

- Ongoing communication updates, such as what's happening or sharing successes
- Including nonparticipants in feedback
- Aggregating data and presenting to key decision-makers and stakeholders on a monthly basis
- Addressing concerns swiftly
- Connecting the program to compelling annual events, such as demonstrating how the program supports environmental activities on Earth Day or communicating how productive participants were on a snow day

Deliverables for the Launch stage are:

- Pilot results
- Training results
- Initial results of success metrics

Some of the key risks of this phase are:

- Change in leadership
- Data isn't captured adequately
- Results or successes aren't shared or encouraged widely
- Team loses steam and pilot program becomes the final step

6. *Measure*: Your next key steps are measuring success and reporting it to the program team. This is with a view to scale the program in a way that makes it accessible and ubiquitous to the rest of the organization. To ensure your organization is realizing the ROI or other metrics first envisioned in the Investigate phase, you'll need to develop, track, and evaluate both enterprise-wide and individual metrics of success. Successful organizations track not only the success of

the implementation but also the correlation to performance outcomes, including financial benefits to the organization, customer satisfaction, and productivity. You need to carefully manage expectations; communication and promoting successes are critical in this phase.

Some of the key activities in this phase are:

- Measuring success metrics
- Recurring reports to senior management and the rest of the organization
- Highlighting and communicating success stories and best practices

Deliverables for the Measure stage are:

- Documented success stories
- Documented success metrics

Some of the key risks of this phase are:

- Lack of management involvement reviewing metrics
- Inability to capture data
- Success stories are not communicated
- Tools for enterprise-wide sharing are not made available

7. *Leverage*: The best organizations don't stop once programs are implemented; they use the information gathered in the Measure phase to make adjustments, course corrections, and improve performance. With initial success, the program can be rolled out to the broader organization. Organizations can capture unanticipated benefits. For example, if executives launched Workshift to save on real estate costs, they may realize benefits for talent acquisition and retention. Finally, organizations can evolve the program into a real competitive advantage by searching for ways to optimize, redesign communication-based work processes, or differentiate themselves in the market.

Some of the key activities in this phase are:

- Promoting the program
- Ongoing communication, such as sharing data or telling the story

	1 Investigate	2 Discover	3 Design	4 Engage	5 Launch	6 Measure	7 Leverage
Purpose	Identify if Workshift will benefit the organization	Gathering data, perform gap analysis, & create strategy	Turn strategy into a detailed Workshift plan	Socialize plan, communicate & gain buy-in	Execute Workshift plan	Monitor, measure, and evaluate launch	Begin broader implementation of Workshift
Key Activities	• Research • Find case studies • Elevator pitch • Socialize	• Gather data • Define end state • Id. & validate assumptions • Gap analysis	• Census building • Program charter • Communication plan • Training req. • Select team	• Census building • Communication • Storytelling • Myth-busting	• Communication • Aggregate data • Address concerns • Connect to compelling events	• Measure success metrics • Sr. Mgt reviews • Communicate & share info	• Promotion • Ongoing communication • Tracking • Identify opportunities
Deliverables	• High-level business case • Committed sponsor or champion	• Clear business case • Strategic goals • Complete gap analysis	• Program charter • Program resources • Success metrics	• Communication plan • Stakeholder (SH) analysis • Change Mgt plan • Case studies	• Pilot results • Training results • Initial metric results	• Documented success stories • Documented success metric results	• Implementation plan • Comm. and change mgt plans • Document benefits
Key Risks	• No credible info • No Sr. mgt. sponsor • No "airplay"	• No timely data • Conflicting end state • Lack of buy-in	• Pockets of resistance • Limited time • Inadequate plan	• Nobody signs up • Mgt resistance • No attention from Sr. Ldrs.	• Change in leadership • Lack of data • Results not shared • Team loses steam	• Lack of mgt involvement • Lack of data • Slack of communication	• Program stalls • Not linked to ongoing biz strategy • Results not reviewed

Figure 1.2 Stages of Workshift development.

- Tracking the results
- Identifying additional opportunities to capture benefits (financial and nonfinancial)

Deliverables for the Leverage phase are:

- Implementation plan for the broader organization
- Revised communication, training, and change acceptance plans
- Documented benefits (beyond initial program goals)

Some of the key risks of this phase are:

- Program stalling, fizzling out, or fails to expand
- Program is not linked to ongoing business strategy or performance management systems
- Results are not reviewed, or are reviewed inconsistently

Wherever your organization sits on the spectrum, this methodology will help you chart a way forward (summarized in figure 1.2). What we have consistently found, in both working with organizations implementing Workshift, and the numerous case studies of how it is being realized across many industries and with organizations of varied sizes, is that these are the essential ingredients and steps that set up conditions for success. Having clarity and understanding the challenges that exist in an organizational culture will yield additional insight into where more efforts need to be directed. All organizations struggle with aspects of evolution and change, but a key differentiator today is characterized by rapid technological innovation coupled with a growing mobile workforce that has raised the ante for organizations to evolve in ways never seen before. If organizations don't evolve, the outcomes are clear: they will lose competitive edge and the most talented employees.

In the next chapter, Investigate, you will learn the steps required to understand how Workshift can be realized in your organization.

CHAPTER 2

Investigate

The only real voyage of discovery consists not in seeking new landscapes but in having new eyes.

—Marcel Proust

"We simply needed to reduce our costs," one HR director told us. She worked for a nonprofit organization that consisted of just over five hundred employees. Turnover was low, most of the employees had been with the organization for several years, and people were very satisfied with their management and their jobs. But like many organizations, they were under pressure to reduce operating costs. They already had an older telecommuting policy in place, and over half of the employees worked from home on a given Friday. The organization didn't receive any financial benefit from telecommuting employees. It was just another retention tool to ensure their highly talented employees remained happy.

"We have a lot of office space for our relatively small organization," she explained. "In fact, it's become almost an expectation that when an employee reaches a certain milestone in their tenure, they will get their own office."

The real estate cost to maintain these individual offices grabbed the attention of senior management. Soon, senior leaders were asking HR and facility management to look into expanding the organization's telework policy and redesigning the workspace to consolidate space. A value proposition was created, a plan was developed and approved, a program manager was appointed, and tasks were assigned. Workshift was now in full gear.

It's important to note that many large, complex initiatives start with relatively simple ideas. You may already be well aware of the drivers and benefits to work flexibility: attract and retain top talent, continuity of operations planning, reduce real estate and travel costs, improve employee productivity and quality of life, reduce carbon emissions, and for federal agencies in the United States, comply with the TEA of 2010. We have found through our research and working with clients that most organizations are rarely propelled to Workshift by more than one or two key drivers. This is not to say that an organization can't realize all the benefits. However, leaders are usually faced with a specific challenge, and change eventually becomes, or is at least part of, the solution. Although we hope leaders in the future will embrace Workshift as a key strategic aspect of their business, for now we recognize that one desired benefit usually becomes the spark that will ignite this effort.

The objective for the Investigate stage is to pique interest, start generating support, and start putting things in motion to get to the next phase. This stage should be relatively short in duration and culminate with two key deliverables: a high-level business case or value proposition and an executive sponsor. Before you can reach this point you need to evaluate your organization and answer the following questions:

- Does the organization have any existing policies in this area (i.e., telecommuting, telework, or flexible work arrangements)?
- If existing policies are in place, who and how many people are using them, and what is their feedback?
- Are there informal, unsanctioned, or undocumented practices occurring in the organization?
- Which groups within the organization are likely to be the biggest supporters? The biggest resisters?
- Are competitors leveraging similar policies or practices?
- What are your organization's current biggest challenges (according to the executive team)?

Understanding the Current Situation

Every organization has a slightly different starting point, depending on their prior experiences, industry, organizational culture, and management objectives. To gather initial executive support, and justify further effort, you need to take all these factors into account. First, understand your organization's history with past efforts. Many organizations have telecommuting, telework, or flexible work policies either buried in their HR department or used actively within some part of the organization. The policies may have been created for one-off situations that surfaced but were never fully adopted or socialized in any meaningful way. Some policies may be outdated and hard to find, while others may be readily available even if not used actively. With the policy in hand, the first stop is usually the HR department to understand the history, who originally initiated it, how it was accepted, when it was rolled out, and who may be currently using it. Although we strongly advocate that any change to employee work arrangements be a decision and initiative driven by the business leaders, we often find that it is led by HR and considered an HR program.

Regardless of whether a policy is in place or not, you'll want to identify any pockets of employees or teams that are already informally working virtually. Interestingly, most companies we work with divulge that they are aware of many employees working from home or at a remote location part-time, working modified schedules, or at least accessing information and performing their jobs while not on an official work site. If possible, informally interview the employees and managers you find who are engaged in these unsanctioned or unofficial practices. Seek to understand the genesis of these work arrangements and why local management approved or at least allowed it to occur. More importantly, find out why management continues to allow these practices. The information gathered will help build the business case and provide relevant, firsthand success stories and benefits. You may also discover benefits you may not have considered on your own.

In addition to understanding the benefits people are already realizing from informal practices, you will also begin to learn the types of managers, employees, teams, or departments that are more likely to adopt the new program. In the Discover stage, you will conduct a much more rigorous assessment of the culture and subcultures that may exist in your organization, but in the Investigate phase you are taking a quick, broad snapshot of the organizational landscape to determine groups of potential supporters and challengers. Later, you can develop specific strategies to turn resisters into adopters, but it's still helpful to understand the barriers up front. You can proactively address these concerns in your business case to start breaking down the walls early.

As important as it is to understand the policies and practices within your own organization, don't forget to examine what other organizations are doing. Look outside and inside your industry and geographic area to understand best practices, lessons learned, successes or failures, and who is best in class. Understanding industry trends may indicate the necessary changes to keep employees, comply with legislation, become more customer responsive, or be more flexible—all of which link to Workshift. It's unlikely that the challenges confronting your organization are unique. Others have likely grappled with similar issues and have found, or at least experimented with, solutions. Benchmarking provides an opportunity to shorten the learning by standing on the shoulders of others.

Knowing what the competition, or the rest of the industry, is doing can help support your business case. No one wants to get left behind or miss an opportunity that could translate into competitive advantage. However, don't be afraid to directly contact your competitors. The world is moving from competition to collaboration and more often we are seeing "competitors" share their best practices with each other.

In Calgary, a city heavily weighted in the oil and gas sector, we discovered several mid- to large-sized companies in the Investigate stage of their adoption. After months of meeting with decision makers from these companies, some very similar trends started to emerge: First, these organizations were all talking about implementing Workshift, but resisted being the first mover. Executives feared losing employees to the competition if the employees revolted against the new work arrangement. Second, none of them were very aware of what the others were doing. Lastly, their compelling reasons for adoption were to attract and retain top talent rather than realize real estate savings or capture quick financial savings.

It certainly seemed that if they were willing to get together and share their experiences, challenges, and plans, the acceptance would accelerate, leading to swifter adoption. In September 2011 they did just that. Calgary Economic Development sponsored an

Energy Roundtable to bring in these companies. Six of the seven companies invited attended, providing approximately 20 employees from senior positions in real estate, HR, and IT. In the end, the participants were thrilled to have the opportunity to collaborate with their "competitors." They discovered ways their peers had overcome challenges. They openly shared their experiences and fears. The participants from the Energy Roundtable claim they are still in touch with one another and use each other as resources.

The Energy Roundtable is one example of how you might be able to creatively tackle some of the myths, challenges, and presumptions. There is also another key reason to conduct benchmarking. Talent is more fluid than it was a decade or two ago. Much has been written about the Millennials, or Generation Y, the newest generation in the workforce. One of the interesting statistics about Gen Y is that they are likely to have five different careers and work for 20 employers during their lifetime.[1] This is quite different from the norms of the Baby Boomers, who expected to work for the same organization their entire career, or the Gen Xers who may switch companies a few times over their career but feared being perceived as "job hoppers." Gen Y is helping to change workforce dynamics, making it acceptable to cross over from companies or industries. And with this constant infusion of new talent comes new norms and work practices. Employees who have adapted to the new work environment may find it difficult to go back to a traditional work arrangement. Employers may find themselves losing the talent war if they can't keep up with the trends their employees have become accustomed to.

Building the Business Case

With a thorough understanding of the current situation, the team can begin to build the business case. Like any initiative, the business case typically contains the benefits and costs, and creates a compelling reason for undertaking an endeavor. It can be used as a marketing tool within the organization to help sell the concept to leaders and employees. The business case needs to clearly answer the question, "Why should we do this?" However, a good business case should go beyond just benefits and risks and offer a vision for the future, links to other strategic imperatives within the organization, a comparative reference with competitors, potential alternatives, and even failure criteria to help identify if the initiative has veered way off course.

It's important to point out that the business case is a living document. Keep in mind that the organization is in the earliest stages of implementation during the Investigate phase. It's likely that many of the details won't be flushed out until the gap analysis is complete in the Discover stage, and this may make the authors of the draft business case feel like they are in the proverbial catch-22. Resources will be needed to complete the due diligence required in the Discover stage, but the needed support won't be authorized until organizational leadership is sold on the idea. To overcome this paradox, those responsible for the business case should think of this as an iterative process. If necessary, use the information on hand or that is quickly available to unlock the interest among decision-makers, which will allow more research. In today's world of abbreviated information and sound bites, we have seen business cases that were no more than a couple of PowerPoint slides. This is probably not adequate to justify a full organizational commitment to Workshift, but it's a step in the right direction. With this in mind, here are some of the key elements found in any business case:

- *Compelling reason*: The most important objective of a business case is to create a compelling reason to justify the effort and answer the questions *why should we do this?* and *why do this now?* This is sometimes referred to as "the pitch." Proponents can start with identifying the problem they are trying to solve, the so-called "burning platforms" within the organization, or leaders' "hot buttons." Is the real estate team looking for new space to accommodate your growing organization? Does the organization need to downsize facilities? Is the HR team struggling with the costs of attracting and retaining new talent in a tight workforce market? Perhaps your company is facing lean times and there are fewer ways to hold on to the team who are accustomed to annual bonuses that won't be coming this year. Or perhaps your leadership is looking for new ways to leverage the latest technology that is infusing the workplace. Workshift then becomes a solution. One of the most compelling aspects of this type of program is that it can address myriad business challenges facing executives of the twenty-first century. You can start by making a list of the key challenges facing your organization and start mapping out the solutions. Then, identify which solutions may be enabled through new work arrangements.

Workshift should also link to other strategic objectives or the mission/vision of the organization. For example, a health-care provider may have a mission statement such as "Provide exceptional health care with a team of professionals, dedicated to excellence and the highest quality patient experience." Workshift may link directly to that vision by seamlessly connecting professionals and patients anytime, anywhere in country. As an enabler to the overall mission, Workshift offers an alternative, virtual milieu for helping to achieve that seamlessness in an effective and efficient way.

History or previous experience with telework or similar implementations can also be included. This may be necessary if the organization's past efforts at telework or flexible work options have failed. You should consider carefully why this time will be different. Alternatively, if there has been some success and now is an opportunity to expand on those results, then that should be highlighted as well.

- *Vision/end state*: At a high level, what is vision for the future state? Where do you want the organization to be? Providing some thought around what leaders should expect in the future if they move forward can help make the effort more tangible. Implementations can take months, quarters, or even years. Countless tactical decisions will be made along the way. Sometimes short-term decisions are made at the expense of long-term results. The business case serves as the reference point for the business for all decisions related to the program. Leaders can tie smaller or lower-level decisions back to the vision and ensure correct choices are made.

Those developing the case should include a general, realistic timeline of when the organization will reach the future state. High-level metrics of success should be identified to measure whether the organization has reached its intended objectives. Even if baseline measurements have not been fully collected, it is helpful to identify how the team plans on tracking end results. Also, it is helpful to include some basic level of failure criteria or boundaries so leaders can identify if the effort has gone off track.

- *Benefits and costs*: Most executives are focused on the monetary benefits and costs of the program. ROI is the one universal financial metric that is used by organizations to determine whether an initiative is worth the effort. Obviously, the benefits may be hard or soft, but all the benefits to the organization should be captured and communicated to leadership (see table 2.1). For example, hard benefits could be classified as those that directly impact the income statement or budget. Facility savings due to a reduction in lease expenses, commuting/travel cost reductions, or reduced talent acquisition costs (i.e., less expenses or commissions paid to third-party recruiting firms) could all be considered hard or tangible benefits. Soft benefits may include productivity increases, reduced absenteeism, or increased employee satisfaction. As an aside, we've witnessed heated discussions around categorizing certain benefits as hard or soft. The simple test is if you can actually reduce your budget by the identified amount or reinvest it into the business. For example, some managers wish to include productivity as a hard benefit. Although leadership may be excited at increased levels of reported productivity, how does this impact the bottom line? Is headcount reduced, more product produced, or more transactions completed that will generate more revenue? If so, then it can be classified as hard savings. Otherwise, if you can't directly tie it back to your organization's financial statements, then it is likely a soft benefit. Furthermore, it may be necessary to split costs between direct costs (e.g., you contract with an outside vendor to provide training) and indirect costs (e.g., the time you "borrow" from other employees to help participate on the core program team). The team should engage finance professionals to validate and help provide some rigor around any financial analysis.
- *Scope*: In project management methodology, scope usually refers to all the work that is required to deliver the end result and the conditions under which it will be delivered. To oversimplify, how big is the change anticipated to be and

what are the boundaries? Will the implementation impact employees globally, regionally, or confined to one particular work site? Again, in future stages you will build this up in greater detail and discuss things such as phased approaches or pilots, but you initially need some starting point and expected impact to help prepare the leadership team. Additionally, any known constraints or assumptions should be documented. Constraints may include any restrictions from cost to specific job requirements that necessitate a traditional work arrangement. Assumptions can also include open questions that still need to be answered or clarified in the Discover stage.

- *Risks*: By understanding the barriers to change you can begin to identify areas that may impact the scope, timeline, or resources needed to implement. For example, if you know a specific department or function that is willing to work in new ways but the tools and technology they currently use most likely won't support the new arrangement, then the issue should be highlighted early on even if you are yet to complete the due diligence to select the most appropriate tools. You are helping to set expectations at the start of the process that moving to a new work arrangement will require an investment in technology.

Lastly, the business case should include the risks for *not* implementing the change in work. There is always a cost for maintaining the status quo or doing nothing. Will competitors pass you by? Will operating costs keep rising and erode your business? Will employees begin jumping ship? Preventing an undesirable future can be just as persuasive as achieving the ideal state.

Table 2.1 Benefits to the organization

Hard benefits	*Soft benefits*
• Real estate savings • Facility energy/maintenance cost savings • Reduced travel costs • Reduced talent acquisition costs • Headcount reduction • Reduced employee relocation costs • Reduced IT infrastructure costs • Reduced insurance costs • Tax credits (if applicable)	• Improved employee satisfaction/greater work-life balance • Productivity • Reduced absenteeism • Reduced carbon footprint • Disaster recovery/continuity of operations • planning • Reduced commute times

Once the draft business case is created, it can be socialized or at least reviewed by others for input or suggestions. It is never recommended that the business case is developed in a vacuum or by just one individual. We recommend sharing it cross-functionally. Let finance, HR, asset management, operations, and others play an important role in shaping it.

The completed draft can also be used to develop an elevator speech—the concise, direct summary of what Workshift means and what it will do in your organization. Think about who the target listener or listeners are and what you want them to remember most. Next, think about the key value Workshift will bring to your organization, the key benefits people will care about most. If you are recycling a former policy or restarting a program that is off track, be prepared to add in something that will explain what is different this time. You can also add in any immediate or short-term goals, the potential timeline, and what you'll need to get it done.

As a last tip, it's okay to personalize your business case. Your business case may be full of facts, figures, and financials, but many people have trouble relating to statistics alone. It's no secret as to why many marketing professionals will provide anecdotes, stories, or testimonials over presenting lots of research or data to make their case. Stories are very powerful, and because they reach us at some emotional level, they tend to stick with us more than numbers. You can use this to your advantage by incorporating case studies or anecdotes into your business case. We have found that in many organizations, many workers are already engaging in an unsanctioned form of new work practices. Highlight some of their positive experiences, or conversely, find workers who are working in traditional ways but could benefit greatly from the change and tell their story. Either way, you'll add a human component to the business case, which will help sell the concept internally.

Creating a Change at Blue Cross and Blue Shield of Massachusetts

Karen Kelly of Blue Cross and Blue Shield of Massachusetts, Inc. (BCBSMA) is very familiar with the process of building a business case and gaining support. Kelly, a 24-year veteran of the company, helped lead the effort for flexible work practices and the company's e-Working program. In 2005, business leaders reached out to HR to request a flexible work program. Other local health plans had a number of nurse work case managers working from home, making it difficult for the case management area within BCBSMA to recruit top talent. Job candidates were already asking if working from home was allowed. When they learned that work-from-home options were unavailable, many candidates sought employment elsewhere. HR approached IT to help develop a solution to allow employees to work from home, and ultimately help the company regain its edge in recruiting. Initially, the idea was met with resistance by IT. There were limited resources, budget, and time to justify the effort. Kelly, directed by the VP of financial services, was assigned to manage the effort and develop the business case.

Kelly began working cross-functionally with HR, IT, finance, and business leaders. The team took a holistic look to identify the areas that could benefit from flexible work options. They compared the costs of housing employees, and their equipment, in office buildings versus the cost of purchasing equipment to be used in home offices and then factored in potential gains in productivity. The team also learned that in the prior year, a handful of employees within the claims division began working from home. Although the program didn't expand beyond the few employees, it provided a useful proof of concept. Armed with data and analysis, Kelly and her IT partner approached various leaders to present the business case.

"This was very much a grassroots approach," Kelly explained. Although they had senior management support, leaders did not want to force managers to change the way they managed their teams unless the managers were comfortable. "We had a 'birthday cake' culture. Every week you would see people in the office celebrating a birthday, promotion, or work anniversary."

Organization Quick Stats

Name: Blue Cross and Blue Shield of Massachusetts, Inc. (BCBSMA)
Industry: Health insurance
Year founded: 1937
Description: BCBSMA is a community-focused, tax-paying, not-for-profit health plan headquartered in Boston that is

committed to working with others in the spirit of shared responsibility to make quality health care affordable. Consistent with its corporate promise to always put its 2.8 million members first, BCBSMA is rated among the nation's best health plans for member satisfaction and quality.
Headquarters: Boston, Massachusetts, United States of America
Region: Regional
Number of employees: Approximately 3,500
Revenue: N/A (not-for-profit)
Website: www.bluecrossma.com

Leaders wanted to maintain high levels of engagement and did not mandate the program, which was internally known as e-Working. The e-Working program meant that an employee would permanently give up their assigned office space to work from home. Yet, leaders were also able to incorporate flexible work arrangements even though they did not adopt e-Working.

"We support that. We encourage that through our disaster recovery program. Many associates work from home a few days a week or whenever their schedule allows," Kelly said. "When we have a storm and the roads are dangerous we can shut down the building but not the operation. If people work from home a day a month then they will get used to it."

By presenting the business case at various levels in the organization, many leaders and teams bought into the program. Over time, the business started realizing the ROI and the business case continued to build. The company was able to consolidate office space as a result.

"We looked at the first three years and thought we would have 450 deployed," Kelly told us. "Seven years later we have 700 people in the program. We've also saved about $8.5 million per year in real estate expense or cost avoidance. We would need a full, large building just to house people if this program ended."

Gaining Commitment and Sponsorship

Building a strong business case and identifying an executive champion for change is essential. Executive sponsorship is a powerful statement that shows other organization leaders a serious commitment is being made to changing the workplace culture. Some champions may be assigned sponsorship from higher management, while others volunteer because of their passion or interest in the effort. Regardless, leaders should be clear on what the role of champion is, why it's so important, and the champion's responsibilities. A champion's main role can be described by the following six responsibilities:

1. *Communicate the case*: Although the business case may be a collective effort, the champion or sponsor is the chief evangelist or executive face of the initiative. The champion should emphasize the risks of maintaining the status quo, highlight opportunities, paint a compelling picture of the future state, and link the initiative to the business strategy to make it relevant to the organization. In other words, the champion has to tirelessly push the business case through all levels of the organization.
2. *Set expectations*: Champions play a critical role in ensuring other leaders or groups within the organization are aligned and driving closure for any gaps in support. The champion should reiterate the need to achieve the desired results and communicate the high-level metrics that will be used to measure results.
3. *Lead by example*: A good champion doesn't let others simply opt out. The champion leads the way by demonstrating desired behaviors. When necessary, the champion makes visible sacrifices for the initiative's success and clearly shows that Workshift is a high priority. Sponsorship is not delegated down to lower levels; the champion legitimizes the change through personal influence.
4. *Reward the right behavior*: The champion should have the power to influence behavior by positively recognizing and rewarding desired behavior changes. Communicating successes across the organization will also help create the needed momentum. Conversely, the champion can visibly provide consequences for behaviors that do not support the change.
5. *Resolving conflict*: As coordinators or program managers advocate and drive the move to the virtual office environment, challenges will always arise. The champion is the person the program team goes to for help, whether it is dealing with

difficult stakeholders, clarity on organizational priorities, or resolving budgetary gaps.

6. *Mitigating risk*: The champion should proactively understand how the initiative impacts other areas within the organization. Risks should be identified and the champion should anticipate the disruption to the organization in relation to the needed changes. The champion can reach out to other organizational leaders to counter any resistance or work through challenges.

In this early stage of development it may be hard to find the ideal champion that can fulfill all the requirements mentioned above. Consider if your organization was approaching Workshift with a grassroots approach. You may want a champion from the top executives of the company, but they aren't paying you, or the idea, much attention. Obviously, you want to reach high up in the ranks since senior leaders inherently have more decision-making authority, may be more widely known, or can more easily allocate resources to support the cause. But what can you do? Think of developing a sponsorship network or several supporting sponsors. You may have to search for the leader who best suits your needs now to get to the next stage. Any leader below the targeted executive champion who understands the impact to their organization, department, or function and is likely to show sponsorship to their teams may be a supporting sponsor. Similar to the executive champion, supporting sponsors must demonstrate the right behaviors through personal example, reinforce the right behaviors in their personnel, and ensure priorities are aligned. Supporting sponsors also ensure information is cascaded down through their teams. You can later exploit this network of support as part of the change acceptance plan or as you get closer to launching Workshift, but in the Investigate stage the focus is on gaining executive commitment. At some point, the champion or sponsor may change, and that's okay too, as long as the new champion can provide adequate sponsorship.

Getting the Right Amount of Airplay

Even with a well-crafted case and some level of sponsorship, many organizations we've worked with still have trouble getting the right opportunity to present the information to senior management. Or, the concept doesn't get enough attention at the mid-levels of management even with senior leadership support. Regardless of the approach, it's likely that proponents will encounter some level of early resistance. In our experience, most organizations don't reject the idea outright. Instead, management demonstrates more passive aggressive behavior by using delaying tactics or simply ignoring it. This can be very frustrating to program managers as they try to gain traction with their idea.

Consider a couple of different tactics to overcome this early obstacle. Often, persistence is the key. When BCBSMA implemented e-Working, it was met with some skepticism in certain business areas. Although top-level executives supported the program, including the CEO, chief financial officer (CFO), and chief operations officer, some VPs and directors were apprehensive. Line managers and supervisors were comfortable with the new program, but VPs and directors wondered how people would get their jobs done. To some, working from home was only done when an employee had a personal matter to take care of and that prevented the employee from participating in meetings or taking calls. Karen Kelly repeatedly went to staff meetings and team meetings to present the business case.

"I was relentless," she said. "Over time, leaders became more comfortable."

If advocates are still not getting much traction with their constant effort to get in front of business leaders, they may need to recognize that leaders at all levels sometimes need to see or feel the pain before acting on it. For example, years ago, when the push for the "paperless" office was the rage, a finance manager we knew was trying to get senior management buy-in on a simple web-based solution that would eliminate the need for many manually created spreadsheets and reports. Although the head of the department publicly claimed to support the paperless initiative, it was clear through her actions and decisions that many other priorities took precedence. After several weeks or trying, the finance manager received permission to get five minutes on the agenda at the beginning of the department head's weekly staff meeting. She arrived in the conference room wheeling in a stack of all the printed reports they were required to produce on a regular basis. The finance manager was only a little over five feet tall and the stack of paper rose just over her head. She only needed to tell the department head how often the amount of paper reports were created and how much it was costing the company annually. Approval was given quickly, with a few minutes to spare.

The case above may be a little dramatic, but it does illustrate a key point. Making the effort tangible can help engage leaders more quickly than a series of PowerPoint slides. That is not to say you should ignore the due diligence in creating your business case and only appeal to people's emotions. However, it is always helpful to make leaders experience the relevance rather than just relying on analysis.

Program managers should also create a sense of urgency to combat any delaying tactics they encounter. The question *why now?* needs to be answered clearly. Again, proponents can make leaders feel the relevance. For example, in one presentation we've seen, picture after picture of empty office cubicles were shown along with financial data that showed the rising facility expenses and how that would impact the overall budget. This helps leaders connect the dots and force some action. Taking this concept further, it would be easy to envision how you could do something similar to tie into the primary objectives of your effort. If your organization is losing talent to competitors, show the raw feedback from employee exit interviews with turnover data, cycle time to replace and retrain new hires, and talent acquisition costs. If the key objective is to improve employee productivity to keep up with increasing demand, a case study following an overwhelmed employee and their daily life, including long commuting times, coupled with data covering the organization and forecast for the future may help. Remember that the purpose of presenting the case in a formal manner is not to inform management or employees, it is to motivate and drive to action. If people don't think the problem is real and needs to be solved now, then they will quickly turn their attention elsewhere.

The Right Time to Implement at TransCanada

It may be cliché, but timing can be everything. Some organizations may not be ready to jump on board quickly and may need time to let the idea incubate. If the organization's leadership pushes back too hard and does not buy into the business case, all is not lost. Future opportunities can arise and necessitate a reevaluation of the concept. A good example is found in the experiences of energy infrastructure provider TransCanada. Rick Coutts, VP of information services, was initially intrigued when he was first approached by another member of the senior management team.

"I remember thinking here was an opportunity to really optimize people's time and see the potential for increased productivity," said Coutts from his office in Calgary.

Four years passed between this initial introduction and when the company decided to implement a new program.

"At the time, we were a pretty conservative company and the concept didn't get adopted. But I kept it in the back of my mind and sometimes you just have to be patient," he said.

With more than four thousand employees in three countries, TransCanada continues to grow exponentially, hiring about five hundred new people every year. With the company's growth and the overall demand for office space in downtown Calgary reaching the critical point, Coutts determined in October 2012 that the time was right to offer a four-month pilot project for employees in TransCanada's IT department. While there was some anxiety around the idea four years ago, that wasn't the case this time.

"I expected only the most bold employees to participate in the pilot project but there was significant pickup, greater than we expected," he said, adding about two hundred employees took part, almost twice what they expected.

Organization Quick Stats

Name: TransCanada
Industry: Energy infrastructure
Year founded: 1951
Description: TransCanada is one of the largest providers of gas storage and related services in North America. The company operates approximately 37,000 miles of pipeline, connecting almost all major gas supply basins in the continent, and controls approximately 10,800 megawatts of power generation.
Headquarters: Calgary, Alberta, Canada
Region: North America
Number of employees: Approximately 4,200
Revenue: Over $8 billion ($CDN) (2012)
Website: www.transcanada.com

Laura Maurer, HR consultant at TransCanada, joined the company just as the team was starting the pilot program. The concept is second nature to Maurer, who as a consultant, worked in a flexible environment for many years.

"For me, this all made sense. It's easy and I understand that world, I understand how it drives efficiency, how it results in real estate benefits, how it makes employees more productive."

Working with Coutts and his management team to implement the pilot project, Maurer offered tools and resources for employees to become comfortable with the changing work environment, including a strong training program, tips, and lunch-and-learn sessions for employees. It's worth noting that the effort did not fall completely on the shoulders of Coutts and Maurer. "Change champions" were deployed to ensure that managers understood the objectives behind the program, how it worked, and what the success factors were.

"In order to be successful, we wanted to define Workshift 'TransCanada style.' In other words, we told employees 'we'll tell you the boundaries and you figure it out.' It doesn't look the same for everyone. And it was important for everyone to understand that a few bumps along the way doesn't mean failure," she explained.

An employee survey in January 2013 found that 83 percent felt the pilot program was successful and 90 percent felt it had long-term potential. Ninety-one percent of employees felt their productivity improved or stayed the same and 94 percent agreed their work-life balance had improved, including an average of one less hour a day commuting. This is not to suggest that there haven't been some minor obstacles. TransCanada is still improving its technology and many employees are still making the transition to a virtual office place.

"I believe it's a behavioral thing. People need to get their heads around a new style of workplace," explained Manfred Eggebrecht, a business analyst at TransCanada and project manager overseeing the test phase. "Our company is growing very fast and within the current confines, there's no way that we have the space going forward."

Coutts says alleviating the crunch on office space is maybe the compelling reason from the business case to support the program, but there were other benefits as well. He cites the potential for increased productivity, better work-life balance, and improved collaboration technologies as other motivators that were components of the business case. As we noted earlier, the business case is an iterative process that continually gets refined as either the business needs change or the expected benefits become clearer.

"My workforce is going to be more diffused. I can see that happening in the next ten years," Coutts said. "Clearly the demand is there and it's going to be more and more possible for people to work whenever and wherever they want."

Putting It All Together

The Investigate stage and the following stage, Discover, overlap in many areas. The work done in Investigate is relatively high-level compared to the granular level of detail uncovered in the next phase. To get the resources or commitment to complete a rigorous assessment of the organization that will eventually lead to a detailed implementation plan, an individual or a small team must first gather enough information quickly to justify looking further. The approval to move forward will be based primarily on how well the team can sell the concept to decision-makers and getting a leader to champion the cause. With this buy-in the team can next determine their organization's readiness and current state, which will help refine the business case and show leaders how far they are from the desired end state.

Stage 1: Investigate—Summary

Key activities in this phase are:

- Research
- Finding case studies within the community/industry
- Creating the elevator pitch, answering the question, "Why would you do this?"
- Socializing the concept internally, formally or informally

Deliverables:

- High-level business case (that demonstrates the ROI value for implementation)
- Committed sponsor or champion willing to take the idea forward

Key risks:

- Not finding enough credible information fast enough to build your case
- Not identifying a sponsor or champion within executive ranks
- Not getting enough airplay to communicate the concept

CHAPTER 3

Discover

An organization's ability to learn, and translate that learning into action rapidly, is the ultimate competitive advantage.

—Jack Welch

If you're in the Discover stage, you've received approval to move forward. The high-level concept has merit and people, whether it is executives, managers, or other employees, want to know more. Now it's time for the deep dive into your organization to understand in detail where the organization stands compared to the desired state. This gap analysis should examine the organization from multiple levels or areas, including business strategy, organizational culture, IT infrastructure, and facility/space utilization. The results of this research can then be used to solidify the business case and become the foundation for an execution plan that will be created in the Design phase.

Strategy Mapping 101

The first step in the Discover stage is to demonstrate the link between Workshift and broader organizational strategy. From our experience, demonstrating this alignment can increase chances of success because it shows how Workshift brings value to an organization by identifying causal linkages between its outcomes/benefits and larger corporate goals and initiatives. In many regards, launching Workshift is analogous to any other initiative or project. Although there is no definable end like most projects (leaders would most likely continue new work practices until it is embedded into day-to-day operations), it should have clearly defined deliverables and a start date, and be likely led, at least initially, by a core team. Therefore, we can leverage the research that has examined the performance of projects that are either clearly aligned to business strategy or not. In one study, researchers compared projects encountering challenges that hindered its success to those that were performing well. Overwhelmingly, projects that had strategic value and were linked to organizational objectives had fewer problems than projects that did not.[1] Many organizations have incorporated the concept of strategic project management, aligning strategic business objectives with project management strategy, to achieve competitive advantage. Using projects as one of the building blocks for planning, organizations create a project portfolio to help achieve objectives. Workshift can become part of this portfolio to enable business strategy.

Volumes have been written on strategy—the importance of developing one and how to do it. Many organizations spend a lot of time and resources on strength, weakness, opportunity, and threat (SWOT) exercises, financial modeling, or other detailed analysis. However, to oversimplify the strategy process, leaders create the vision of where they want the organization to be and how to get there. It starts with the organization's mission and vision statements and cascades down into specific strategic objectives and actions that set the direction for all future planning and execution.

Many organizations understand that creating a flexible work environment is a strategic business imperative, but few are yet to employ a strategic management system to demonstrate causal linkages of it. Ensuring Workshift is tied into strategy or explicitly stated as a strategic objective or action increases chances for success through higher visibility and relevance to management: an important distinction in helping to garner organization commitment and evolve the corporate culture.

Many organizations use a strategy map to visually document the relationship between vision, mission, objectives, actions, and high-level metrics. Strategy maps can also help engage employees and teams at all levels because they can see more clearly and discern how their job or role supports the overall mission of an organization. Strategy maps were an outgrowth of the balanced scorecard framework that uses a combination of financial and nonfinancial categories, including customer or stakeholder, operational, and learning and growth, to capture information in support of an overall mission and vision. They vary from organization to organization and help tell a visual story of an organization, the logic of the strategy, and the important link between strategy formulation and execution. Even if your organization doesn't use strategy maps, the conceptual framework is a useful tool for demonstrating how Workshift can be linked in.

The following two examples (figures 3.1 and 3.2) illustrate how Workshift can support an organization's strategy. The first example is for a health-care provider and the second is for a community bank. Both are fairly generic and an observer, regardless of industry, can see how the initiative is brought in. The objectives outlined in solid circles represent what leaders may develop to support the vision and mission. Objectives outlined with dashed circles may be created without Workshift in mind, but would clearly align and

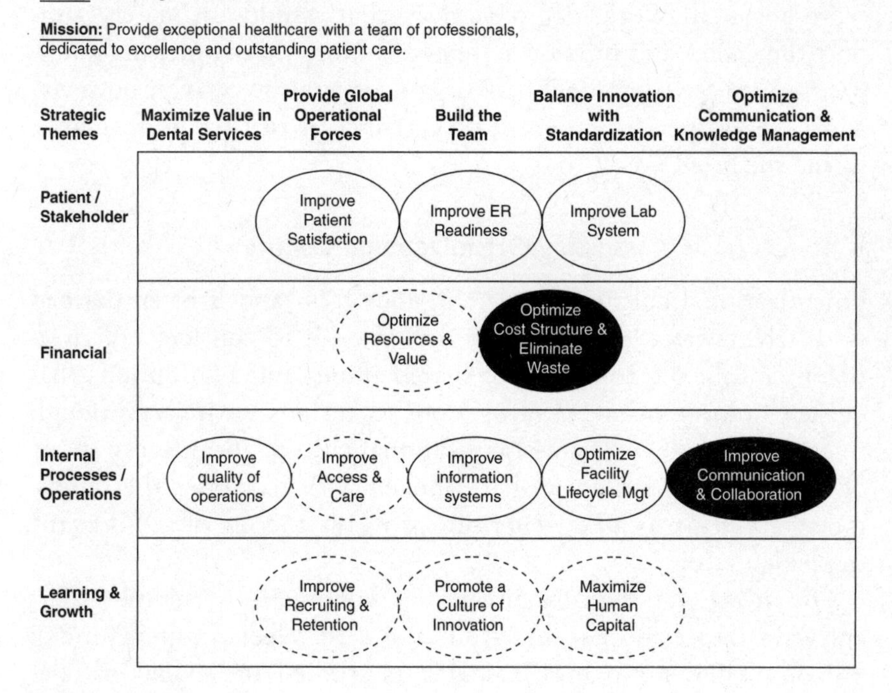

Figure 3.1 Strategy map.

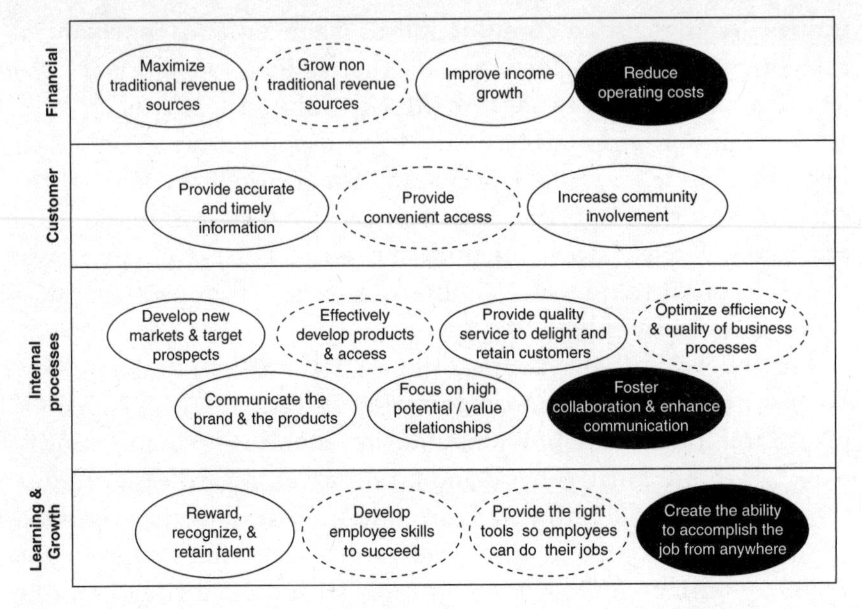

Figure 3.2 Bank or financial services strategy map.

support the stated objectives. Lastly, the objectives filled in dark represent new Workshift objectives that would ultimately support the vision and mission statements. Note that launching a new program doesn't mandate new organizational objectives; however, adding new specific program objectives can further performance in the specified areas.

Assessing Organizational Culture

Organizational culture is an ambiguous term and is often defined in different ways. One common definition is to consider organizational culture the collection of shared values and assumptions that guide employee behavior and actions in various settings. Although research is yet to correlate organizational culture and success, many of the leaders to whom we have spoken with recognize the importance of culture as a key determinant to the success of a Workshift implementation.

Organizational culture influences employees in many different ways. For example, in a study done on telecommuters among Silicon Valley companies, researchers studied the extent of telecommuting (the number of days per week spent telecommuting) on the attitudes and behaviors of employees. The authors found that telecommuters were more committed to the organization and more satisfied than non-telecommuters. However, as telecommuting increased above 60 percent, employee satisfaction and commitment began to drop. Although researchers did not have a definitive answer for this decrease, follow-up interviews and focus groups indicated that the employee attitudes, in part, were the result of senior management resistance. In short, employees were afraid to take full advantage of their telecommuting options if their management valued their physical presence more than telecommuting adoption.[2]

This study also highlights the importance of subcultures that exist within every organization. Although a broad culture may help classify the entire organization, each function, department, or team may have their own distinct culture that supports or, in some cases, runs counter to the corporate culture. For example, executives may support the effort to reap benefits in a real estate savings, but if mid-level managers in a particular department believe face time is a necessity for employees to work well together, then adoption is likely to be slow and painful. This is an important callout since assessing culture may be an iterative process to understand the various groups within an organization and how each may adopt the new work arrangement.

One Company's Telecommuting Program Goes Off Track

In chapter 1, we briefly mentioned the story of the supply chain company that attempted to implement a telecommuting policy. The company was suffering from a high attrition rate, and the HR department responded by launching a comprehensive employee satisfaction survey to better understand why employees were leaving. One of the top issues identified by the survey was poor work-life balance. With full support from the president of the company, the HR team published a telecommuting policy to allow employees greater flexibility. However, even after a fairly successful pilot, the program died out within six months. No one was working any differently than before the survey was conducted.

The program team failed to recognize the importance of organizational culture. Leaders in the organization managed by line of sight. If they couldn't physically see their employees working in their cubicle, they assumed their employees were not working. To illustrate how deep this concept was ingrained into the organization, one employee told us the story of the conversation he had with his manager during his annual performance review. The employee was disappointed he received a below-average rating. He approached his manager with detailed facts and figures about what he accomplished during the year.

"The perception that I have, as well as some of the other managers, is that you don't work any harder than you have to," the manager explained.

"What do you mean?" asked the employee.

"Well, you're always the first one out the door at five o'clock."

With a culture that put such a high price on presence within the office space, what employee would dare risk telecommuting if they wanted career advancement? Despite the executive support, managers at various levels clearly didn't buy into the new work arrangement. The company possessed the technology to allow employees to work from anywhere but it didn't matter. The tools and technology would never be used if managers were resistant to the very concept of employees working where they couldn't be visually monitored. The program team failed to address the cultural factors up front and the program ground to a halt.

The program lay dormant for a few years until something very dramatic happened. A hard-working employee became ill and continued to work in the office despite her condition. (Given the type of organizational culture, this perseverance was actually looked on favorably by many managers.) When the employee finally decided to visit a doctor, she was diagnosed with the H1N1 virus, commonly known as "swine flu." Panic ensued within the employee population. More and more employees began calling in sick as many feared they had become infected. Quickly, executives and the HR team dusted off their telecommuting policy and managers now began to accept employees working from home versus the alternative of losing employee productivity altogether. When the crisis was over, many managers realized that their operation could continue without the need to be physically co-located with one another. They were commended on their flexibility. Finally, the organization turned the corner and realized the benefits of having the ability to work from anywhere.

The story above highlights an important point. Organizational cultures are hard to change. Without a traumatic experience or some external event that forces a rapid response, changing a culture requires lots of planning and preparation. However, this is not to suggest that all program teams will face an uphill battle. Organizational culture can also be a positive influence and accelerate adoption. An example of how organizational culture can propel Workshift is Trend Micro.

Trend Micro: Using Organizational Culture to Propel the Virtual Work Environment

Trend Micro is the global leader in cloud security. Headquartered in Tokyo, Japan, the company's executives work virtually from across the globe. Eva Chen, CEO and cofounder of Trend Micro is based in Pasadena, California, while the CFO, Mahendra Negi is located in Tokyo. The company's chief technology officer is in Germany, the chief information officer is in Taiwan, and the chief marketing officer is in Albuquerque, New Mexico. Other top executives can be found across Asia, North America, and Europe. With an executive team that works seamlessly in the virtual world, it's no surprise that the entire organization lives and breathes the work-anywhere concept.

"I was blown away when I came to Trend Micro," Dan Woodward, VP of US Marketing, told us. "Through technology and an amazing work relationship, our executives get [work objectives] done on a daily basis and that cascades down to the rest of the organization."

Organization Quick Stats

Name: Trend Micro
Industry: Technology
Year founded: 1988
Description: Trend Micro is a global leader in cloud security, developing Internet content security and threat management solutions that make the world safe for businesses and consumers to exchange digital information. Trend Micro is recognized as the market leader in server security for delivering top-ranked client, server, and cloud-based security solutions that stop

threats faster and protect data in physical, virtualized, and cloud environments.
Headquarters: Tokyo, Japan
Region: Global
Number of employees: 4,942
Revenue: $1.2 billion ($USD)
Website: www.trendmicro.com

Woodward, like many of the people we spoke with, made the hard transition from a traditional office, where he was expected to be in everyday from 8 a.m. to 5 p.m., to a home office. Prior to working at Trend Micro, he didn't consider working from home a positive thing. He enjoyed being able to reach over and talk to someone, to collaborate, or get a conference room to draw on a white board. Although he has a home office that is physically separated from the rest of his home in Salt Lake City, he admits that he initially had to deal with the daily distractions of balancing work and family matters. For Woodward, the transition took about six months.

What made the transition easier for Woodward and many other employees is the culture within the company. Interestingly, Trend Micro was the only company we came into contact with that actually had a chief culture officer.

"[Chief Culture Officer] Jenny Chang, one of the company founders, is charged with maintaining the drumbeat of where we want to be and who we are as human beings, not just as a company," explained Woodward. "Steve Chang, another one of our founders, highlights over and over that you should be your best self, whether that means working in an office or working virtually."

This intense focus on maintaining an organizational culture that values employees and *how* they work, not *where* they work, permeates into activities at various levels within the company. For example, when job candidates are interviewing for a position within Trend Micro, interviewers assess skill sets and experience, but they also evaluate how the candidate will fit into the culture and the ability to work within a virtual team.

"Curiosity is not enough," Woodward said, explaining that Trend Micro's intense interview process specifically looks for experience working in virtual teams and a potential employee's propensity to work without being in physical contact with their manager or other employees. Not all employees work remotely, but working in an office location is typically an employee's decision and not mandated by the company.

When new employees are hired, they attend an orientation and are introduced to the technology used at the company that will enable them to work remotely, along with guidelines for how the technology should and should not be used. Unlike some other companies we spoke with, Trend Micro does not require specific virtual team training. The company has guidelines instead of set rules, and expectations are set by managers. Working virtually becomes a natural aspect of an employee's job.

"When the employee is successful, the company is too," Woodward stated.

The Elements of Organizational Culture

Given that organizational culture may be a barrier or an enabler to adoption, leaders need to first assess the current culture before developing their implementation plan. Several tools and methods already exist to help evaluate organizational culture. Some use scoring mechanisms to rate the current culture compared to the desired state. Our approach doesn't attempt to quantify the culture as much as to create a picture of the organization's readiness that can then be compared to its approach. For example, if the organization tends to be very collaborative with decisions made cross-functionally due to a matrix-style reporting structure, then driving a program with a top-down approach, as an edict from senior executives, may not yield the best results. This understanding will feed the Design phase and help determine the specific actions leaders need to take. Whether you are assessing the entire organization or a specific team within the organization for a pilot, we recommend using the following questions to better understand how decisions are made, how employees work together, and the values that are most important.

Decision-making:

- Describe the management style (e.g., results focused, customer/employee centric, or coaching/coordinating).
- How are decisions made (e.g., top-down, consensus, or a collaborative approach)?

- How much autonomy do employees have in the decision-making process? Specifically, how much autonomy do managers at various levels have (are mid-level leaders expected to seek approval from higher levels of management)?
- What accountability do employees/leaders have for their decisions?
- How are decisions rewarded/reprimanded? Are employees/leaders encouraged to take risks, or do they fear repercussions and will wait for decisions to be made by higher levels of responsibility?
- Do formal policies govern what people do, or do leaders have flexibility? If formal policies exist, what is the process for how they are developed and administered?

Working styles and teamwork:

- Are teams within the organization competitive with each other?
- What is the level of trust between employees? Is it expected or is it earned?
- How do employees typically communicate with each other?
- Are employees geographically dispersed, and if so, how does this impact performance?
- Do employees typically work with the same team members or do they commonly work cross-functionally within new groups (hierarchical versus matrix)?
- How is feedback from employees gathered and how is it commonly used?
- Do generational differences impact team/organizational performance? What is the generational mix within the organization?

Values:

- What is the glue that holds the organization together?
- What are the ideals that best describe the organization?

If similar initiatives have been attempted in the past or are currently in place, leaders can delve into more specific questions, such as:

- Are Workshift initiatives tied into position descriptions for which people are being evaluated against (for management and supervisors)?

- Does the organization have a Workshift center of excellence or centralized team that helps develop strategy, policy, or evaluate technology?
- Does the organization identify program eligibility for each position?
- What initiatives are being promoted to encourage alternative work options?
- Is Workshift tied to agency employee engagement initiatives?
- Are specific user needs identified when planning for Workshift?
- Does your continuity of operations plan integrate Workshift?

Again, these questions are to increase a leader's understanding of their organization culture and it is not intended as an all-encompassing list. It can be used as a platform to probe deeper in some areas that help identify potential roadblocks or areas where focus will be needed.

Assessing Technology and IT Infrastructure

Before BCBSMA implemented their e-Working program, they had to assess the needs of their e-Workers, those workers who would permanently work from home and no longer have a dedicated office space. Hardware, accessories, software, and security all became important considerations."We tried to get them the same setup they had in-house," Karen Kelly, program manager for e-Working, said. "I had a computer, monitor, keyboard, mouse, and a printer. When I deployed home, I received new equipment because the company wanted to make sure I had reliable equipment. e-Workers also received a router as an extra layer of security. The router is programmed to the associate but they don't have the key and the wireless is shutoff. We use a soft phone and ensure they have high speed internet. However, e-Workers have to provide their own furniture and we also provide them with a safety compliance checklist."

Obviously, Workshift is enabled by technology. IT leaders within the organization should be part of the discovery process as early as possible to understand current capabilities and the IT requirements needed to reach the desired state. However, before specific technology solutions can be discussed, planners and leaders should answer a few basic questions regarding the business needs of the organization, such as:

- Where will employees commonly work? For example, if one of the key business drivers behind the organization's initiative is to reduce the corporate real estate footprint, will employees be expected to work from a home office or a satellite location? Alternatively, the organization may retain its physical office space and need employees who are mobile, traveling to client sites or working from the road. It might be necessary to segment employee groups based on specific mobility or telework requirements. Your IT leaders may refer to these *end points* and cover not just the location where people work, but also their devices and how they connect to the network.
- What type of work activities do employees perform on a daily basis? Again, different employee groups or departments may have different needs. Analysts who need access to large amounts of data will have different needs (i.e., high bandwidth requirements) than a sales rep who is constantly on the go. Understanding job requirements will also help IT planners understand what level of access people need. Some may need full access to the network and services, while others may need only limited access to services or access for a temporary time period.
- How will people work together? Communication and collaboration is essential to ensure virtual teams perform well. A variety of voice, video, collaboration, and sharing tools are available in the market today. Putting budget considerations temporarily aside, leaders can use the information obtained in assessing the organizational culture along with specific job requirements to start thinking about how they *want* virtual teams to work together.
- What type of information do employees work with? Security is always a top concern for IT leaders. Planners should consider the sensitivity of the information used to perform an employee's job. Access to applications and information, whether it is financial data, HR applications, or classified documents for government employees, may require additional layers of security or alternative solutions.

- Will employees use their own devices? A big trend in today's marketplace is BYOD (bring your own device). About one-third of US companies allow an employee's personal device (i.e., a smartphone or laptop) access to the network.[3] Although BYOD has become a hot buzzword, many companies have allowed *unmanaged devices* some level of access for quite some time. *Managed devices* are usually those that are issued by the organization (i.e., a company-owned laptop or smartphone) and in the active directory. When a user logs in the user typically receives a statement about the organization's compliance policy. That same managed device may regularly receive security or software updates and can be tracked to ensure compliance with organizational policies. Many employees already have access to some basic services, like viewing their company's email account from their home computer, an unmanaged device. With the explosion of mobile devices, there are a multitude of new end points to consider. This will add many new considerations, such as what types of devices, apps, and access will be permitted, what level of tech support the organization will provide, and who will pay for the device.

As a starting point, planners can begin by answering the questions above and filling in a simple matrix, mapping needs to requirements. Table 3.1 represents a very simplified view of this

Table 3.1 Needs vs. Requirements matrix

Employee Group	*Needs*	*Requirements*
Executives	• Redundant, fail-safe connectivity • Reliable and secure access • Rich-media experience (i.e. HD video)	• Rich portfolio of plug and play endpoints • HD video, HW/wireless phone
Operations (Home-based workers)	• Consistent, 24/7 connectivity • Reliable and secure access • Basic video and phone requirements	• Access to email, collaborative tools • PC-based video • PC or hardware-based voice
Field sales (frequent mobile workers)	• Connectivity from multiple devices • Reliable and secure access • Mobile video and voice requirements	• Mobility, smartphone, access at home, hotspot, 4G

approach, and other columns can be added to identify potential threats or risks as well.

Once basic business needs and requirements are mapped out, planners can dive deeper into the current environment by asking these additional questions:

- What foundation is already in place (i.e., firewalls, multifactor authentication, remote access services, remote messaging services, document encryption, etc.)?
- What are the current IT security guidelines and policies that cover working off-site (or telework or mobility)?
- What mobile devices are employees currently using for work (i.e., laptops, tablets, smartphones, etc.)?
- How many devices are deployed (as a percentage of the employee base or mobile population)?
- What collaborative meeting software is being used (i.e., LiveMeeting, WebEx, GoTo Meeting, etc.)?
- Is video used and how is it used (webcams to telepresence)?
- What technologies or tools are used to share information across functional silos?
- Are there established common infrastructure layers to support Workshift (network security, device management, etc.)?
- Is there a standard acquisition process for mobile technology?
- How flexible is the organization to incorporate new devices?
- Is there a BYOD policy?
- Do you provide standard mobile data management (MDM) security protocols to allow employees to use their own privately owned devices?
- Are MDM initiatives linked to the overall IT strategy?
- Do you have some sort of "sandbox" environment to create and develop prototype solutions to address mobility needs/strategy?
- What type of tech support is offered to mobile or work-from-home employees?

Figuring out the technical requirements to support the virtual workplace can be a daunting task for most leaders. "One size fits all" solutions usually won't suffice, and planners need to consider multiple scenarios based on the various needs of the organization. It can't be overstated to include IT leaders in discussions at the very onset. They cannot be brought in after the fact. However, it is worth pointing out that business leaders need to lead the discussion. While talking with some IT managers, more than a few have pointed out that in some cases Workshift began as an "IT-only" discussion. For example, the IT department at one organization began to investigate how they could accommodate the growing use of employee-owned devices on the network, yet it wasn't possible to complete the task without first understanding job roles, business processes, and business leader expectations.

Assessing Physical Office Space Needs On-Site

The motivation for launching a program is not always driven by a need to better utilize or reduce an organization's real estate footprint. However, the program will impact the volume of space required to support the workforce and how the space that is required will be used in the future. Therefore, it is important to study the existing workspace design, available resources, and space utilization in order to develop baseline data for effective space planning activities after the implementation.

For decades office space has consisted of a sprawling labyrinth of cubicles, private offices, and conference rooms. In recent years, employers have started to move away from "cube farms" and migrated toward workplace designs that provide spaces and resources that better match the work styles and interaction needs of employees and managers.

WellPoint: Assessing and Realizing Corporate Real Estate Benefits

Executives in many companies have noticed that as more and more employees are working occasionally from home, traveling more frequently, or working increasingly flexible schedules, the need for dedicated workspace assigned to every employee is no longer necessary. For example, real estate executives for WellPoint, a leading provider of health-care services in the United States, sensed that the space on a corporate campus was being underutilized. Although the workspaces were almost fully assigned and were full of files, computers, binders, and other signs of life, there were few people actually in the space. The WellPoint team hired an architecture firm to study the campus and quantify how many people were actually using their workspaces. The architecture firm spent two months walking the entire campus at various times of the day and combined this census data with information from WellPoint's security system to create a profile of space utilization. What they found was that although the space was almost fully assigned, 65 percent of the employees assigned to the space did not enter the building during the research period. As a result, when it was time to renew their lease for space on campus, they were able to save millions of dollars annually by only leasing space that was needed for true on-site employees, and configuring on-demand space for others.

Organization Quick Stats

Name: WellPoint
Industry: Health care
Year founded: Formed in a merger in 2004
Description: WellPoint is one of the nation's largest health benefits companies, with more than 36 million members in its affiliated health plans and nearly 67 million individuals served through its subsidiaries.
Headquarters: Indianapolis, Indiana, United States of America
Region: National
Number of employees: Approximately 350
Revenue: $60.7 billion
Website: www.wellpoint.com

On-demand space, also known as hoteling or hot-desking, has become an increasingly popular method for reducing office space needs by better matching workplace resources with employee work styles. Many organizations have tackled the issue of better aligning work process and space resources by deploying more open office designs that allow workers to sit together at tables and collaborate more effectively. The primary goal common in all of these and other workplace strategies is to break the one-to-one relationship of a single employee to the exclusive assignment of space. Workshift becomes the key component of enabling the seats within a workspace to begin to support more than one employee.

Hoteling: Reservation-based seating assignments
Hot-desking: Reservation-less seating assignments (first-come, first-serve)

Determining Office Space Needs

In order to design space that effectively supports employee and seat count ratios that exceed 1:1, planners need to understand how people work and then leverage that information to design work-space that supports work flow and interaction needs. Similar to the IT assessment discussed in the previous section, planners can start by thinking through business requirements with the following basic questions:

- Who uses the office space and why? If it's helpful, categorize the types of employees who may use or need it. Keep in mind that this may be related to the subcultures identified as part of the organizational assessment. At Trend Micro, Dan Woodward broadly segmented employees into three groups. The first group included teams that work naturally in the field, such as a field sales representative, support engineer, or even some of the marketing team. These employees want to be where the customer or partner is. For Woodward's marketing team in the United States, approximately 55 percent work in an office location and 45 percent work in the field. The second group included those with a unique synergy that works better when employees are physically together. Transactional based teams, such as an inside sales team, thrive on the energy of one another. For example, when a sale is made, a team member may ring a bell and the rest of the team gets motivated to make additional sales. Lastly, there may be a strategic reason for a physical office location to have a presence in an identified area. For high tech companies like Trend Micro, having a physical presence in Silicon Valley is a necessity.
- How do people work within the office space? For example, do people regularly work as part of different project teams and need a place to collaborate? Are workers traveling frequently and just need a working area to touch down?

- What type of work is done in the office place? Are client/customer meetings held, which require dedicated conference or demonstration rooms? Are confidential conversations held or sensitive information used (i.e., HR discussions with employees), which require audio privacy areas? Is training conducted on-site, which requires a training area or room?
- How often do people use the facilities? Current tools and surveys available in the marketplace today will help measure the utilization of buildings, conference rooms, and offices that can help determine the total workspace needed.
- What type of equipment do employees use or need? Different from an employee's home office or remote location, employees need the organization's facilities for more than just a copy machine or scanner. The organization may require high-end, immersive telepresence or other sophisticated hardware.
- Is the organization trying to ensure compliance with Leadership in Energy and Environmental Design (LEED) requirements or other green initiatives?[4]

Linking Workshift to LEED

LEED was developed by the US Green Building Council (USCGB) in 1998 to encourage green technology in building design, construction, operations, and maintenance. Compared to conventional buildings, LEED-certified buildings are intended to not only use energy more efficiently but also provide healthier work environments. In turn, these healthier work environments can lead to higher productivity and improved employee welfare. According to the USCBG website, LEED certification is internationally recognized and stretches across 135 countries. Many local governments offer incentive programs to promote LEED certification in the form of tax breaks or credits, grants, low-interest loans, bonuses, reduced fees, and/or expedited permitting.

For commercial buildings, the LEED certification is based on a 110-point rating scale that evaluates the building across several categories including water and energy efficiency, indoor environmental quality, innovation in operations, and sustainable sites.

Workshift can have a direct impact in achieving LEED certification. For example, in the Sustaining Sites category, points are given for "Alternative Commuting Transportation." The requirements of this category include:

> *[Reducing] the number of commuting round trips made by regular building occupants using single occupant, conventionally powered and conventionally fueled vehicles.For the purposes of this credit, alternative transportation includes at a minimum, telecommuting; compressed workweeks; mass transit; rideshare options, human-powered conveyances; carpools; vanpools; and low-emitting, fuel-efficient or alternative-fuel vehicles; walking or bicycling.*

Furthermore, by optimizing the physical workspace due to the Workshift initiative, other LEED certification categories may be impacted indirectly, such as emissions reduction, occupant comfort, innovation in operations, or building operating costs.

After business requirements are understood, specific details of the design can be discussed. Changing the workspace will require planners to consider numerous details from lighting to power outlets to phones. Spaces may have multiple uses (i.e., rooms used alternatively as conference rooms and offices) and may require furniture that are on wheels and can be moved around easily. Personal storage areas for an employee's personal belongings and access to shared equipment may also be considered.

In addition to the changes you consider in the physical workspace, keep in mind that these changes tie closely to the changes you are trying to make in the organization's culture. Don't assume that employees will immediately accept or adapt to the planned design. In the Design stage you will be developing a comprehensive implementation plan, including many of the change management activities necessary to transform the organization. This will have to incorporate actions to help employees adjust to any dramatic changes in the physical office space. For example:

- *Communication*: Your communication plan needs to be holistic, including changes not only in work arrangements or technology, but also in workplace design. Having witnessed some organizations change their office layout, it was surprising how some employees resisted. People may become accustomed to their personal workplace and the value proposition you provide to employees needs to include the reasons why the organization is making the change and how employees will benefit from the new office arrangement. One best practice is to set up a portion of the building or floor in the new format, if possible, so employees can see and experience what they are moving to. Also, allow enough transition time and a chance for employees to ask questions or familiarize themselves with the new environment.

- *Establish and enforce ground rules*: If your organization is moving to a hot-desking model, establish and communicate rules and policies. For example, if there are only so many closed offices or conference rooms, how will you prevent employees from squatting all day long and preventing others from using them? Some companies successfully use room-booking software to address the management of space on a daily basis. What about employees who intentionally leave personal belongings behind for days at a time in order to preserve their spot? Who mediates disputes between shared resources? All these issues can be fairly common but problematic if not thought through in advance. You may also need to decide who will monitor the office environment, how this will be done, and how rules will be enforced.
- *Prepare for contingencies*: When planning for an unassigned seating environment, it's likely that facility managers have calculated (usually based on average office occupancy over a period of time) how much space is needed. Think through what happens if the facility maximizes or surpasses peak occupancy. This could have unintended consequences, such as employees reserving space "just in case" but never use it or relocating themselves to areas where they shouldn't work. Overflow areas may be needed, or active monitoring of unused reservations might be in order.

Assessing Physical Office Space Needs Off-Site

Whether an employee's off-site location is their home or some other location, often referred to as the "third place," it is important to consider an employee's workspace requirements for locations away from the office. A majority of the organizations we spoke with leave it up to employees to establish their own workspace at home, with the exception of providing employees basic tools (i.e., a laptop or phone). However, there are exceptions.

One company we spoke with provides employees with equipment and reimburses them for office-related expenses based on their participation level in the company's telework program. "Full-time" participants were defined as those employees with no assigned space on-site and "part-time" participants were those employees who still had assigned space, but the space was shared with other employees.

The company's real estate team identified the company's cost for rent and occupancy, and then interpolated the cost for an average workstation and office. What they found is that the cost to provide employees with basic furnishing and equipment for their home office was a fraction of the cost spent for rent and occupancy on their on-site workspace. Based on this information, the program team established the following provisioning guidelines for employees:

Full-time teleworkers
Desk (if required)—$600
Chair (if required)—$450
Two-drawer lateral file (if required)—$300
Paper shredder—$100
Multifunctional printer—$400
DSL/cable modem installation (if required)—$100
Second phone line installation (if required)—$50
Cables, lamp, etc.—$150
Laptop and virtual private network (VPN) access (if required)—$2,400

Part-time teleworkers
Paper shredder—$100
Multifunctional printer—$400
DSL/cable modem installation—$100
POTS (plain old telephone) line installation—$50
Cables, lamp, etc.—$100

In addition, the company provided the following reimbursement for business expenses:

Full-time teleworkers
High-speed Internet/phone—$100 month/annual allowance $1,200 (maximum)
Sundries (offices supplies, printer cartridges, etc.)—$300 annually

Part-time teleworkers
High-speed Internet/phone—$100 month/annual allowance $1,200
Sundries (offices supplies, printer cartridges, etc.)—$150 annually

Many employees used to years of working in a traditional office setting may find it difficult to adjust to working from home, not because they miss the social, physical interaction with other employees, but because they may not have the equipment or furniture to create a productive work area. Providing these resources may be a cost-effective way to ensure that employees have a work environment at home that is both conducive to completing their work and ergonomically correct. Some employers may balk at the potential costs of providing additional equipment to employees, arguing that the cost the employee saves in commute and other expenses associated with working on-site more than compensates the worker for any incremental costs incurred with working at home. Regardless of the company's approach to provisioning employees with home office equipment and expense reimbursement, it is important to understand the impact of the approach on cost savings and the impact on employee productivity and safety. At a minimum, leaders can find a way to share best practices to help employees with questions and help optimize an employee's personal workspace at home.

Putting It All Together

By now you see the large leap between the Investigate and Discover stages. To oversimplify the difference, the Investigate stage is the internal sales pitch and explains why the organization should pursue a new way of working, while the Discover stage starts to uncover how the organization will get there by examining all facets of the organization from its culture to its technical and physical infrastructure. Organizations use the Discover phase to uncover useful readiness assessment data that is an important step in laying the groundwork for creating a way forward. While the Discover stage may be resource intensive and somewhat time consuming, if done correctly, it can pay big dividends, helping leaders build and launch Workshift. The information gained will be essential for leaders to create a robust implementation plan in the next stage, Design.

Stage 2: Discovery—Summary

Key activities in this phase are:

- Gathering data
- Clearly defining the end state
- Identifying and validating assumptions
- Performing gap analysis (IT and organization)

Deliverables:

- Clearly defined business case
- Demonstration of how Workshift links to broader strategic goals
- Completed gap analysis

Key risk:

- Not collecting organizational data in a timely manner

CHAPTER 4

Design

Design is not just what it looks and feels like. Design is how it works.

—Steve Jobs

After the organization data unearthed in the Discover stage is collected, it is then used to help inform and craft the next phase, the Design stage. The data gathered in the Discover stage provides a platform for meaningful conversation, positions the ROI, and will help you avoid common pitfalls associated with adoption.

During this phase, leaders create an operational plan for deployment by not only sourcing data gleaned in the Discover stage but also tailoring a program that creates a way forward, taking into account the unique characteristics of an organization. However, before that can be achieved an important initial step in this process involves consensus building and achieving leadership alignment.

Without creating a value proposition and focusing efforts on achieving strategic alignment among stakeholders, the program runs the risk of being short-term and misunderstood as a trend that will fade away as target participants are reluctant to embrace it. This is particularly true if the value proposition isn't clearly defined as containing strategic business benefits. Too often, telework and flexible work initiatives are positioned as employee benefit programs instead of a wholesale change in the way business is done. Employee programs can be easily discarded or cancelled with the change of leadership, while initiatives that are part of a corporate culture are more widely accepted as a larger business imperative.

But how can alignment be achieved, especially in an organization that may bring together leaders with different mind-sets about the value of changing culture?

Building a strong platform, business case, and ROI, and identifying an executive champion for change is essential. Executive sponsorship is a powerful statement that shows other organization leaders a serious commitment is being made to changing the workplace culture. In helping to create alignment, the executive sponsor (and others working with them or the program team), needs to understand the multifaceted ways that Workshift impacts the bottom line. Demonstrating the ROI, where executives can see how directed efforts and resources positively impact corporate HR, IT, sustainability, and real estate goals, can establish a strong and important foundation for building a coalition of support.

As discussed earlier, the development of a business case can be prompted by one or more pressing business needs. In one example, Eagle Professional Resources, one of Canada's largest staffing firms, established a Workshift initiative initially to achieve real estate cost savings.

Creating the Business Case at Eagle Professional Resources

Morely Surcon, the general manager and VP of Western Canada who led the initiative, felt that Eagle needed to accommodate growth when office space was becoming too small. However, Surcon discovered many other benefits that fit Eagle's situation when developing the business case and these became the impetus of the plan to implement it into their business model in a more robust way. To accommodate these needs Eagle invested heavily in best-of-breed tools, software solutions, and technology.

"Workshift was not a giant leap for our company from a practical or conceptual basis," shared Surcon. "However, we learned over the course of the planning and design phase that Workshift was simply not a new technology, nor was it a new business solution . . . but rather that Workshift could be a core part of a new business strategy—one that touches on many facets of our business."

Organization Quick Stats

Name: Eagle Professional Resources, Inc.
Industry: Professional services (staffing)
Year founded: 1996
Description: Eagle is a privately owned and operated professional staffing company specializing in recruiting and placing technology, finance, and accounting professionals, as well as executive and management consultants for contract and full-time positions.
Headquarters: Toronto, Ontario, Canada
Region: National (ten offices across Canada)
Number of employees: 90 employees; 900 contractors
Revenue: Approximately $140 million ($CDN)

Leadership Engagement

Building alignment and leading change are not only about advocacy and making a case, but also involve engaging leaders by framing the right questions that elicit responses in a way where individuals feel their input is critical to making progress. This form of engagement energizes and motivates people by inviting idea sharing. To do this, an executive sponsor might ask: What would this look like in our organization? What processes need to be refined or established to support that shift? What challenges do we need to overcome and how do we do that?

The data gathered during the Discover stage should be used in these kinds of conversations as a basis for discussion and exploration about possibilities with the leadership team. The Discover stage data should serve as the foundation for all discussions as it develops the baseline need for change and the associated data to support such change. This is the business case that should guide all future conversations and should provide a strong business case for adoption of an alternative work arrangement. Without it, leaders tend to flounder and programs rarely get adopted in any meaningful way.

Leaders can create a more aligned executive team by closely understanding feedback and asking the team what experiences and skills they bring to the table to help manifest change. The process of engaging leaders as an inherent part of building alignment should never be underestimated as an important part of designing a program. Taking these steps in the Design phase can result in the rest of an organization being more apt to internalize and adopt a strategy that brings the program to life.

> Eloise Moodie, MA, change management expert: "Workshift presents to the organization an opportunity for numerous benefits. The trouble is people tend to fear the unknown. Leading the change to Workshift is like leading any transformational change—the first hurdle is helping people to share the vision. Actively engaging key stakeholders at the inception of the change process is the key to building buy-in and adoption of the vision."

A Cultural Shift

We strongly believe that what has been missing from conversations about Workshift are the ways in which it has a broader, more significant impact when it's presented as a cultural transformation initiative and a way to conduct business that's not led by a silo initiative from HR, facilities, or IT alone. An inherent part of the Design stage needs to account for the numerous organizational benefits that cut across departments, engages cross-functional teams, and meets organizational goals. Organizations that embrace the cultural underpinnings are more likely to see the Design stage as much more than just a policy or a charter to create a program.

Gaining Executive Support at USDA

One example of a broader effort that clearly demonstrates executive sponsorship and leadership alignment comes from the United States Department of Agriculture (USDA), a large Federal agency with 29 separate mission areas, with headquarters in Washington, DC. Tom Vilsack, the secretary of USDA, has been a strong champion of the TEA of 2010 by tying it to the agency's cultural transformation initiative, an effort that has played a key role in helping USDA implement the power of flexible/remote work across the agency. On a monthly basis, a cultural progress report is developed for management review. Senior leaders and managers are held accountable for the implementation of the telework program goals and reporting results. Mika Cross, the work-life program manager responsible for USDA telework implementation shared that the cultural progress report is seen as the "ground truth" highlighting what people out in USDA field offices are doing to track telework participation and what eligibility numbers actually are. Data from the cultural progress report are used by Secretary Vilsack to assess performance of the leadership team, who are then in turn held accountable for their part in successfully implementing telework in the field.

When organizations like USDA make Workshift a strategic business imperative, one that is inextricably tied to evolving corporate culture, the chances of longer-term success for designing and implementing a program increase significantly. This is an important differentiator for any organization serious about changing its culture and accepting changes in how, when, and where work is done.

Organization Quick Stats

Name: United States Department of Agriculture (USDA)
Industry: Public Sector; US Federal agency
Year founded: 1889 (founded in 1882 but not given cabinet status until 1889)
Description: The USDA is a Federal agency within the US government responsible for developing and executing federal policies on farming, agriculture, and food. It promotes agricultural trade and production, works to assure food safety, protect natural resources, foster rural communities, and end hunger in the United States and abroad.
Headquarters: Washington, DC, United States of America
Region: National
Number of employees: Approximately 106,000
Revenue: N/A (2011 budget of approximately $132 billion)

Establishing a PMO or Project Team

Identifying a project team or project management office (PMO) is also an essential part of the Design stage. It answers the questions: Who will drive the initiative? Do they have the motivation to make it successful or are they doing it off the end of their desk? How will it be structured, managed, and evaluated? Ensuring that a cross-functional team of influential leaders come together to prioritize the initiative is a critical step in this Design phase as it helps create the right governance structure and augments individual and team participation and collaboration. But what does that look like?

At one end of the spectrum, a project team can consist of only one or possibly two employee champions. At the other end, there can be an established PMO with a mission of starting up flexible work programs across many divisions and business units while serving the dual purpose of becoming a repository of information, tools, and resources for distributed teams and leaders. In the case of Eagle Staffing, once a business case and vision was established and agreement from senior management was secured, the Design stage commenced.

"The biggest question was where to start?" admitted Morely Surcon. This is often a question many leaders face.

One example of where to start comes from the United States General Services Administration (GSA), also with headquarters in Washington, DC. GSA created a telework PMO to help design and implement a telework strategy agency-wide. This PMO was responsible for telework program sponsorship, program management, project management, and workgroups to help facilitate a comprehensive telework implementation process. GSA was given six months to start up a telework PMO and was successfully able to do so through the commitment from executive leadership. Steps taken to establish this PMO included the need for nominating and creating the PMO team, preparing policies, tools, processes, and templates, developing a PMO master plan, and conducting a kickoff PMO session. As an organization, GSA is known for best practices in successful implementation of flexible work and space utilization. GSA has been a champion of the TEA of 2010, and is widely recognized for their Workplace 2020 initiative that has helped evolve telework and telecommuting toward a concept of mobility: "The ability of individuals enabled by the ubiquity and robustness of information technology, and progressive workplace policies, to work freely within and outside the office."[1]

While some organizations, like GSA, committed to setting up a PMO and have the backing and resources to do so, other

Table 4.1 Eagle Staffing Workshift policy

Purpose and outcomes	Describes intent behind the program and goals to be achieved
Definitions	Includes examples of Workshifting, such as flex work, telework, mobile work, and compressed work weeks
Operating guidelines – Working hours – Work locations	Guidelines that outline an employee work schedule in a given week, and work locations. Identifies when an employee must be accessible and through what technologies
Responsibility: —Directors —Managers —Employees	Details on how time and attendance, accrued leave time, or overtime is tracked by directors, managers, and employees
Agreements	A formal acknowledgment between an employee and employer that outlines the tenets of the agreement. Includes safety issues pertaining to designated work areas at a remote site
Tools	Identifies which tools will be made available by the organizations for the employee to use at a remote site. Can include requirements related to collaborative technologies, IM, video conferencing
IM/IT/BYOD security policies	Identifies what corporate-owned equipment will be used by the employee, organization security policies to be followed, security technologies to be employed and followed, and any BYOD policies related to use of personal devices during any work hours or for completing work
Communications	Clarifies expectations for communications with managers, teams, and employees
Training	Identifies what kinds of synchronous or asynchronous training opportunities are required/available to the employee

organizations may not be ready to commit more significant resources to a robust initiative. In these instances, the need for creating a project team, one that is comprised of senior leaders and stakeholders, cannot be overlooked as a condition of success. A project team in the early phases of discussions may opt for initially developing a policy. A policy identifies how flexible workplace practices will be available to employees and what the requirements are of managers and employees. A template for a policy can be seen in table 4.1 from Eagle Staffing.

Program Charter

This team, whether it's comprised of one or two people initially from an organization with a grassroots approach or whether it's established as a larger PMO stemming from a top-down approach, will be responsible for developing a program charter. The charter differs from a policy as it is a road map for understanding the scope of work, deliverables, expected outcomes, success metrics, and change management the key players—the project team, PMO, and stakeholder/champions—are responsible for.

For Eagle Staffing, a key step in their Design stage was the creation of a detailed project charter for their pilot and implementation. This document included details on the project's vision, goals and objectives, expected outcomes, scope, timelines, assumptions, risks, and budgeted costs. The charter also identified a project team and listed each team member responsibilities; and it included a sign-off page for key project sponsors and company executive. Eagle understood that without the support and active participation of the executive team, the project could be jeopardized. A well-designed and managed program requires feedback from stakeholders including employees on a regular basis and is also a component of success.

"It is important to note that the Project Charter was not a static document, meaning that as the rest of the planning documents and details were finalized, we learned new things and identified new opportunities, issues and dependencies that required the Charter document to be updated and modified," shared Surcon. "The process was not linear, but iterative... the planning and design package *came together* and *evolved* rather than being completed one document at a time."

High-Level Success Metrics

Organizations on all levels of the spectrum benefit from the value of high-level success metrics to answer the following questions: How are we doing? Is our program/initiative successful? What are our outcomes? Metrics monitor the ongoing progress toward meeting goals and can unearth more efficient ways of executing a program that results in improvement and change. They also protect the program in the event of leadership or organizational changes. Nobody wants to cancel a "winner."

These metrics should be established with the leadership team as the initiative is developed. Historically, organizations launched these type of initiatives without really understanding what they wished to measure, or worse, how they would measure what they thought was important. Impact metrics are essential to understanding and communicating the value of a program that has been designed and deployed.

One of our favorite anecdotes is the organization that wishes to benchmark productivity increases as a result of Workshift, but can't tell you how they measure productivity of their employees today! Ideally, the same performance metrics should be applied to employees working in traditional office settings and employees working in the virtual workplace. Then, any increases in performance of virtual employees can be attributed to the program.

It's important to ensure that the selected metrics are important or valuable to the organization and tie back to the business case. Leaders should revisit why they are considering the initiative and what value it will yield. There is no point in measuring something that no one cares about. Leaders should identify the end results expected and then determine how the results will be measured.

The "how to" measure conversation can vary greatly from organization to organization. In one client engagement, "productivity" was defined as billable hours increased by 5 percent as a result of the program. In this case, the client measured this monthly and so tracking a change was relatively simple. In many organizations, however, impact metrics are still evolving. In a report by IBM, among the companies that consider flexibility essential to their business strategy, only 50 percent measure the impact of flexible work practices on business performance.[2] Among companies that do measure impact, many report using an average of three measures to track their success, including employee satisfaction, facility cost savings, and utilization rates.[3] Organizations are paying closer attention to the bottom-line savings Workshift provides, which encompasses a broader discussion on the myriad levels of metrics that can be tracked around productivity, ways in which efficiencies are achieved through technology, utilization of space, and corporate sustainability goals, among others.

In one example of measurement, USDA is interested in how telework achieves costs savings as it pertains to real property savings. USDA has 92 million square feet of leased space across the department and the agency is tracking metrics on space, whether it's being utilized or underutilized. As we have noted earlier, to be most impactful, metrics need to be aligned to larger corporate objectives that impact broader goals pertaining to HR, Information Management or IM/IT, real estate, and sustainability. Outcomes and measurement data will provide powerful examples of how Workshift has helped to achieve these goals.

Pilot Selection

Bringing Workshift more formally to an organization is typically done through a pilot project or program. Pilot programs test the efficacy before a full rollout to other areas or before a stronger commitment is made to embed it into a culture. A pilot approach establishes a framework, attempts to minimize organization risk, and often tempers management fears about the effects on employee performance. Often, a business area is chosen to pilot a program where a number of suitable positions have been identified as conducive or eligible for implementation.

Interestingly, we had a number of organizations tell us that they can sell the concept of Workshift by calling it a pilot but then confess, "We call it a pilot in case it fails, but if it's successful we will just keep doing it."

Table 4.2 illustrates how Eagle Staffing approached the development of a pilot program and implementation:

Table 4.2 Eagle Staffing program charter for pilot

Project charter	As discussed above
Metrics framework	Outlines the performance metrics to be used
Training plan	Defines all the training components and their owners
Survey documents	Eagle decided that they would complete pre-, mid-, and post-pilot surveys with their staff and managers to determine the level of Workshift success and acceptance
IT enablement review	Summarizes existing technology, completes gap analysis, and makes recommendations for improvements/new technology
HR policy document	Updated company policy for Workshift
Employer/employee agreement	Sets out rules for participation and defines performance metrics expectations (this is individualized by role within the organization)
Communications plan	Identifies communications required and pairs it to the timelines in the charter
Measurement tracking/reporting	Shares approach/methodology overview

Automattic: Building Flexible Work Practices From the Beginning

Companies that approach Workshift from an au naturel standpoint find that they do not need to design and implement a pilot a program to create a flexible work culture. These are organizations that experienced growth around the model of a remote workforce from inception. Many technology-focused organizations are known for flexible work practices and Automattic, a web-publishing company behind the WordPress blogging platform is one that stands out. Automattic has been recognized as an organization that has successfully grown a 100 percent remote workforce and employs a number of strategies to ensure that this distributed model works. Automattic employees heavily leverage technology in myriad ways including the ones they sell, blogs. Employees use chat rooms, social media tools, video conferencing technologies, and blogging every day to communicate and collaborate with one another to inspire creativity, innovation, and productivity. This results-oriented model of work has helped cement a corporate culture that has thrived on self-motivation and a decentralized way of interacting and developing an evolving suite of products.

On the topic of employees, Toni Schneider, CEO and cofounder of Automattic, shared that a remote workforce has many benefits including contributing to the quality of life for employees in a way where flexible hours, no commute, and the creation of a personal work environment can eclipse the guilt of being away from the office or missing out on hallway discussions. He has seen that when a company is untethered from a physical environment, the whole world becomes a pool of applicants, and communication tools can be leveraged in more ways. For example, chat conversations can be archived and searched and visible to an entire team, while in-person conversations may be lost as soon as people walk away. Not to diminish the power of social connection, Automattic has long addressed the need for occasional face-to-face gatherings by planning and holding several meet-ups in different countries on a regular basis. Not only do these meet-ups serve as an opportunity for remote employees to work side by side, but they offer an opportunity for teams to work on projects that can be built and launched in a week.[4]

Organization Quick Stats

Name: Automattic, Inc.
Industry: Internet services
Year founded: 2005
Description: Automattic Inc. is a web development company behind the popular blogging platform WordPress.com. Its services include VIP hosting for publishers and start-ups,

VIP support program to provide enterprise-level support for WordPress users.
Headquarters: San Francisco, California, United States of America
Region: Global
Number of employees: Over 200
Website: www.automattic.com

Clearly there is a broad range in how Workshift can be embedded in any organization. While many tech companies are spotlighted for more progressive collaborative work cultures, office designs, and workplace practices, companies that have held long-established cultures based on an older model of work face more challenging, and often intractable, workplace dynamics. These are the organizations that benefit greatly from a well-orchestrated pilot program to begin socializing the concept, and then can execute it in a way where conditions of success can be established up front, and the pilot can be rolled out to other business units in a more iterative fashion.

Position Eligibility

Understanding which positions are more conducive for Workshift, and which ones have not traditionally been, including nonexempt/hourly employees, is also an important part of the Design phase. Organizations need to explore concerns that surface when evaluating eligibility. Recent research offers promising news for nonexempt employees, indicating higher-than-expected percentages of employers offering flexible work programs for nonexempt employees.[5] The same research indicated, however, that among those companies that offered flexible work programs for nonexempt employees, many haven't formalized those programs and policies, opening up employers to potential employment law compliance issues.[6] Organizations that consider how to offer more flexible work options to nonexempt/hourly workers should be looking more closely at the kinds of tasks that are required for these individuals to perform their duties on the job and how to address three key scheduling challenges: rigidity, unpredictability, and instability in their roles.[7] Often these tasks are transactional, prescriptive, and more limited to delivery in corporate settings versus a more flexible, remote setting. While there will always be positions perceived as not conducive to work outside the traditional office place, options around flexibility of start and end times, using compressed work weeks, and looking at what administrative aspects of the job can be done from a remote location should be explored. The ability to create a new culture, one that allows hourly workers to leverage this kind flexibility, even if taken in more limited capacities, will help to bring parity to a program designed with a whole organization in mind.

Workshift is more about evolving a corporate culture than simply designing and implementing a flexible work program alone. Addressing how it is set up to be fair and equitable for both exempt and nonexempt employees will increase the chances for it to be successful organization-wide. This can be tricky when organizations at any point along the spectrum report some managers or supervisors of nonexempt employees are more receptive than others. These discrepancies can result in underlying resentments that pit teams and individual managers against each other. Organizations can address these issues directly through multimodal educational approaches that leverage communications and training to help socialize information and engage employees in conversations about not only the benefits of the program, but also strategies for successfully executing and managing performance in a results-oriented way. Delivered effectively, these programs can help drive behavior change among more resistant employees and managers.

Communications Plan

The need for a communications plan in the Design stage is equally important as the need for manager and employee training. Focusing on and prioritizing performance-based outcomes for work produced versus face time is essential. This is an area that causes trouble for even the more seasoned organizations at times, and it is widely known that any alternative to presenteeism has caused many a mid-manager to hesitate. Because results can sometimes be difficult to define and measure, how managers and employees establish a relationship of trust will be abetted through multimodal communications.

A well-executed communications plan includes multiple ways to communicate how the program is sponsored and supported by senior executives down to line managers. The communications plan can leverage social media and business tools that highlight pilot successes, including individual employee or team stories. Offering continuous bidirectional opportunities to share feedback and solicit input on boards and forums that can address solutions to challenges and conflicts that may occur between employees and managers in managing across geographic distances is essential as well.

The USDA offers opportunities for teleworkers to share their successes through YouTube testimonials and newsletter updates. This agency also conducted a telework road show that was promoted and delivered on the web via an interactive format that included video and live presentations with senior leadership and political appointees who spoke about the challenges and successes of telework. These included YouTube testimonials where employees and managers heard short stories about what telework has meant for them and for their workforce. Mika Cross shared that this dynamic, back and forth communication between employees in the field and administrators helped to create another level of listening and an openness to telework not seen previously within the agency. During those exchanges, USDA managers and employees considered new ways to implement telework within their mission areas on a pilot project basis and assessed perceptions about pilots from this kind of interactive discourse where they may have been resistant before.

The USDA, GSA, and many other organizations develop web-based portals to deliver information and resources on mobile working as part of their communications strategy. This serves as central repositories for information and resources for news and policy updates pertaining to telework or flexible work programs. Surveys are often used to gather feedback during or after a pilot phase. Positive feedback can then be communicated to the larger population to help strengthen the commitment from senior executives.

Quantitative feedback, including eligibility and participation rates, is useful along with qualitative feedback from participating employees. Often this feedback is shared through widespread communications and includes feedback and results from successful remote work stories.

Training

Many organizations are challenged by the need for synchronous and asynchronous training for employees who both manage distributed teams and work in distributed teams. Since the issue of mid-manager resistance to telework is widely known and documented, part of designing a program means understanding where employees and managers' deficits are in creating high-performing teams that can be led from anywhere, at any time. While data from assessments conducted during the Discover phase should give a project team insight into particular issues that confront their organization, when it comes to training, many organizations report that the lack of training around how to manage assignments virtually, build in accountability, track outcome metrics, and leverage tools to keep communication working smoothly are some of the persistent issues that come up time and again in successfully managing remote teams.

It's simple to assume that some form of training will be part of the Design phase. After all, with the rapid pace of evolving technology, employees need additional instruction and guidance on how to leverage collaborative tools effectively, how to troubleshoot hardware and software issues, and learn the systems of tracking and reporting time worked outside of the office in remote settings. While this addresses one dimension of helping employees adapt to a new culture, the essence of a successful training program is far more multidimensional. As shared in many parts of this book, resistance stems from many corners. Some of it is rooted in unconscious biases that managers and leaders bring to the workplace. These biases can range from the perception of how success was achieved individually, often paved by long hours and many years in the office. It can also touch on long-standing gender debates about what success means to men and to women and how that is realized throughout the lifecycle.

In more traditional workplace settings, trust and commitment have often been equated with presenteeism, and lack of trust and commitment have often been equated with being out of the office, and not seen.

This old model of work is still alive and well in workplaces that haven't figured out how to shift employee and manager mindsets toward holding employees more accountable for their performance regardless of location. In these workplaces, office politics is seen as an important part of career success, one that is navigated through face-to-face contact. Some would debate that office politics is inherently a behavioral reality when humans work together in any capacity, remote or otherwise. Unfortunately, in traditional corporate cultures it is still fostered in workplace settings in ways that aren't conducive to creating a thriving culture or increased productivity.

The dynamic shifts in how we work today has resulted in far more distributed leadership and employee engagement, which positively dilutes the amount of unproductive time spent navigating through political issues that stem from lack of trust and internal competition. Peter Senge, a noted MIT professor who developed seminal work with his book, *The Learning Organization*, later defined successful organizations as ones that embrace distributed leadership around four capabilities of a leadership framework. The components include: (1) sensemaking: making sense of the world around us; (2) relating: developing key relationships within and across organizations; (3) visioning: creating a compelling view of the future; and (4) inventing: designing new ways of working together to realize the vision.[8] But what does all this have to do with training? A lot. A successful training program recognizes that the way work has been conducted for so many years in the past deserves attention so that the new way of working is understood as a natural progression of evolving organizations toward ways that create far more productive and rewarding settings. Does this guarantee change? Not always. But it addresses the heart of culture and beliefs that have limited so many organizations in the past. And it's up to leaders, executive champions, and other stakeholders to show resistant employees and managers a way forward and that includes ten essential steps (table 4.3).

Table 4.3 Workshift training framework

1	Address bias	Understand unconscious and micro-inequities in the workplace based on management strategies from the past, how they create resistance in the workplace, and how to evolve them
2	Create vision	Craft a vision for what a thriving Workshift culture looks like (as compared to how work has been conducted in the past)
3	Provide program guidance	Create manager-initiated flexible work programs that evolve flex work requests stemming from employees alone
4	Identify eligibility & participation requirements	Identify changes in competency-based workforce development systems that define the knowledge, skills, and abilities to manage virtual teams in flexible work settings
5	Deal with conflict	Communicate strategies to effectively negotiate conflict with employees and teams in remote settings
6	Develop strategies	Create strategies for leaders and managers to foster trust and encourage strong employee performance and accountability
7	Use collaborative technology	How to use collaborative tools and technologies that are used to promote teamwork and productivity, both nationally and globally
8	Address security concerns	Understand internal corporate security systems and mobile device management policies that ensure data is protected virtually
9	Communicate outcomes & results	Use corporate communications tools and systems that provide real time opportunities for employee, manager, and leadership on sharing successful outcomes
10	Provide various training formats	Provide access to training modules that can be delivered in a synchronous or asynchronous way and can address the myriad additional issues surrounding the deployment of a program

Managing Risk

The risks of not properly designing and executing a program are important to understand. Organizations that have embraced a Workshift culture from the very beginning are typically more immune to some of the risks that occur in organizations that have not yet fully embraced a design and execution strategy. Many of these types of companies lack formal policies and leave decisions up to employees and managers about when and where work is completed. However, in smaller start-up organizations, rapid growth can sometimes present challenges to creating a consistent level of understanding the parameters if remote employees are brought on board without understanding the corporate culture. In these instances, lack of a formal policy can raise unforeseen risks, and misunderstandings about the level of productivity and perceived commitment on behalf of employees may be questioned.

Other risks stem from pockets of internal resistance that can present social and organizational risks. If senior leaders or managers question the value of the program, and don't participate in it themselves, this can present challenges by way of inconsistent messages that are explicitly or indirectly sent to employees who do work remotely.

Researchers at MIT have found two kinds of passive face time employees experience: expected face time, being seen at work during normal business hours, and extracurricular face time, being seen at work outside of normal business hours such as arriving early, leaving late, and participating in after-hours business meetings and dinners. The two forms of face time lead to two kinds of trait inferences or conclusions about what type of person someone is. Expected face time led to inferences of the traits, "responsible" or "dependable," and the deep-rooted history of just being seen at work, without any information about what you're doing, leads people to think more highly of you. When you put in extracurricular "face time" you get upgraded to "committed" and "dedicated."[9]

In organizations where this happens, a program is subject to greater scrutiny and failure because systemic cultural issues work against it in a way that undermines long-term success. Flexible work options are much easier to dismiss or retract when they have not been designed to address these systemic cultural issues or be set up in way that identifies opportunities to highlight the cost savings and benefits and recognize and reward those exemplary employees and managers who are demonstrating how effectively it can be done.

A process to ensure success in any organization requires thoughtful planning and design. This phase cannot be overlooked or minimized. Most organizations need to commit resources—employees and time—to ensure a program is crafted well and cultural considerations are taken into account. If resources are not allocated, chances of success decrease and a well-intentioned idea or plan for creating a more flexible work culture that meets the needs of the workforce is greatly diminished.

Stage 4: Design—Summary

Key activities in this phase are:

- Beginning meetings with key decision-makers for their input and feedback
- Census building and leadership alignment: Understanding WHY are we doing this? What are the key outcomes the organization cares about?
- Selecting Workshift cross-functional team including project sponsor and lead
- Developing program charter including key outcomes, deliverables, measurement criteria, and scope
- Developing communications plan
- Determining training requirements

Deliverables:

- Program charter
- Identified, committed program resources
- Success metrics

Key risks:

- Pockets of influential resistance (i.e., the CFO who "doesn't get why we'd do this")
- Program team does not have time allocated to focus on initiative
- Limited resources focused on planning

CHAPTER 5

Engage

When dealing with people, remember you are not dealing with creatures of logic, but creatures of emotion.

—Dale Carnegie

American self-improvement expert, Dale Carnegie, knew how to deal with people. Over 75 years after he penned *How to Win Friends and Influence People*, it still remains both popular and relevant. As the quote opening this chapter suggests, Carnegie knew that we are all complex, emotionally driven individuals who learn to work together through relationships based on intangible qualities such as trust, respect, and understanding. This may sound a bit fuzzy but it's how organizations work. Conducting a technical assessment of an organization's IT infrastructure to determine its readiness to support a fleet of mobile workers will always be clearer than trying to unravel the network of relationships within an organization to determine drivers of behavior. In many regards, understanding and changing the technical layer to enable Workshift is far easier than changing the mindsets and behavior of the people impacted.

Imagine you are a manager for a large organization. The organization already has the technology to allow employees to work from almost anywhere, whether it's at home, on a client's site, at an airport, or in a hotel. However, you know that the culture within the organization values face time. People simply prefer to be in the same room with their coworkers to work through issues or projects. Senior leadership has signed off on your detailed plan, but are you comfortable putting it into immediate action? What are some of the things you may want to consider before making the first broad announcements? How do you plan to communicate the plan and set it up for success?

If you've followed the previous phases, Investigate, Discover, and Design, then you should have a solid business case, a good understanding of where the organization is, and a well-drafted plan to get to your desired state. Now, you need to create momentum to prepare for a successful launch. Workshift always involves a significant amount of change. Before attempting to implement your plan, think about the *what*, *who*, and *how* of change acceptance. Begin by asking yourself the three key questions below. The questions seem fairly simple, but they will help you keep your focus before developing any detailed change acceptance plan.

- What behaviors need to change?
- Who will need to change and who can influence the change?
- How can the organization make these changes?

Behavior Change at ATB Investor Services

Mike Frederick of ATB Investor Services knows well the challenges of changing behavior. Alberta, Canada-based ATB Investor Services is a financial institution that has over 160 branch offices, serving over 240 communities in the province. Frederick, an accountant by profession, is the chief operating officer with ATB Investor Services in Calgary. He has worked his entire career in an office. And by an office, he means the "standard" definition—bordered by coworkers, he had a space furnished with the usual tools such as computers, printers, and telephones, as well as those things to make the space feel like home away from home, such as photos, pictures, and plants.

Frederick admits he was initially skeptical with the idea of a flexible work environment. For Frederick, his home and his work had always been separated by physical location. He questioned whether he and his employees could fundamentally change where and how they work.

"It's been an adjustment for sure," he said, after setting up his home office in October 2012. "My initial concern was how would people collaborate without the face-to-face time, particularly when we're knowledge workers? But I really believe it's the future for a lot of businesses. From our perspective, it's working very well and the benefits are so tangible."

Organization Quick Stats

Name: ATB Financial
Industry: Financial services
Year founded: 1938
Description: ATB is the largest deposit-taking Alberta-based financial institution. ATB offers retail financial services, business and agriculture financial services, corporate financial services, and investor services.
Headquarters: Edmonton, Alberta, Canada
Number of locations: 160 office locations across Alberta, Canada
Number of employees: 5,363
Assets/income: $32 billion ($CDN) of assets; $195.1 million ($CDN)
Website: www.atb.com

Do you want employees to be productive when they are working from home? Do you want your employees and managers to work together well when they are miles apart in different locations?

Sherri Wright-Schwietz, head of talent and story at ATB Investor Services, said the company began looking at flexibility options to help address the challenge of recruiting top financial advisors in small rural Alberta communities. They considered using technology and installed video conferencing so they could still connect their clients to the best financial advisor in the industry but do it virtually. This prevented the company from compromising on the quality of talent and ended up proving that they could expand this idea to other associates.

In October 2010, ATB assessed and measured how employees were utilizing office space in downtown Calgary. Surprisingly, ATB learned that offices were vacant more than half of the time. It also surveyed employees and asked about their existing work and how they envisioned a flexible work environment. Nearly 50 percent said they already had some degree of flexible work and all said they would prefer one if given the opportunity.

"We learned that many employees were only using their office space as a hub. So in January 2011, we put theory into practice and started a pilot project with 30 employees. We gave them the tools they needed to be successful and effectively work from anywhere they chose," she said. "We called it ATBIS Workplace 2.0."

Wright-Schwietz pointed out that for the program to be successful, and before they could begin rolling it out to employees, a number of things had to happen. Foremost was technology—each employee needed high-speed Internet at their home. The company helped with initial home office start-up costs and then a monthly stipend to help with the additional costs of working at home such as increased heat, electricity, and Internet. Each employee's computer is equipped with Office Communicator, software that features instant messaging, video, desktop sharing, and audio-video conferencing. With the technology in place, the company was ready to announce it to employees and begin a pilot.

Leaders, like those at ATB, have to start the behavior change with an understanding of what behaviors they are targeting and what is the expected end state. Are you asking employees to give up their offices and cubicles and want them to work together in a co-sharing or hoteling workspace? Or, do you simply want employees to use new collaborative tools, such as desktop sharing applications or video conferencing equipment? Thinking about the specific things you want your employees to do differently in the future versus what they do now will help to identify the tools or technologies that will augment those changes And we can't emphasize the word "specific" enough. Don't generalize too much and just hope employees will adopt the new program. List out as many of the specific behaviors that are needed to help reach organizational goals.

Once you have identified the desired behaviors, consider the emotional aspect of the change. We are all creatures of habit, and changing established habits or patterns, no matter what the end benefit, tends to make the majority of us uncomfortable. For example, we once worked with a company that was on the cutting edge of communication technology. When the company's management decided to consolidate some of their corporate real estate

(CRE) by moving from a tradition assigned-cubicle office environment to a flexible hot-desking office space, many leaders assumed the transition would be relatively painless. After all, the company was in the fast-paced technology industry and used to continual change. Employees would adapt quickly to any new changes in their work environment, or so management thought. Employees became extremely vocal in their displeasure in giving up some personal space to become office nomads (at least that was their perception). Facility management and department heads were forced to reevaluate their approach, communication, and time needed to make the transition because of unplanned resistance.

After considering the emotional or personal side of changing behavior, leaders should determine incentives, consequences, and a plan for encouraging the right behavior. Establishing performance metrics will become critical to determine if behaviors are matching expectations.

"It is like NOTHING else out there so it takes people a mind shift before they start to understand the benefits and advantages," Wright-Schwietz told us. "Results-based performance is about setting clear expectations on what results you expect and by when and then the associates owns when, how and where they achieve that. It moves away from 'I was the first one in and the last one to leave' thus I am the super star. We don't care about that. We care about what value you are adding to the business. Our expectations of employees haven't changed but how and where the work gets done has. Our work is results-based so when the work is done, that's how we measure productivity."

Metrics provide timely feedback for employees and leaders and becomes an effective tool to motivate the team to higher performance.

"Feedback is very important amongst the group and certainly there is peer accountability as well," Wright-Schwietz added. "And above all, I trust my staff. I have a team of workaholics who would rather be working than wasting time in traffic, and since we started Workplace 2.0 there's never been any issue with productivity. In fact, they are more productive because they are efficient, motivated and more accountable for their time."

In addition to metrics, training is obviously an important method of teaching or prompting the right behaviors when developing a comprehensive training plan. However, it's important to remember that the training plan is more fluid than rigid and can be adjusted as feedback is received and unidentified issues start to surface. Keep in mind that training may be both informal and formal. BCBSMA used both formal and informal training to encourage the adoption of their e-Working program. Two training modules were developed for participants in the program: Leading Remote Teams and Working in Remote Teams. Initially, all e-Workers were required to attend the Working in Remote Teams training and many of the office-based employees were also encouraged to attend. Eventually, they saturated the employee base with training, with most employees having attended at least one of the modules.

The program manager, Karen Kelly, partnered with IT and conducted some informal training as well. As Kelly presented the business case at many staff and associate meetings, she would demonstrate how to use the technology, such as the soft phone, and how it would make working virtually easier. During these sessions she would also talk about productivity, disaster recovery, and how to work from home.

"For the associates, it was a reality check," Kelly explained. "We wanted to get them thinking about how they would work as an independent worker. We wanted them to identify the potential distractions, like barking dogs or kids at home, and what they would have to do."

Lastly, publicizing success stories internally can help not only to identify desired behaviors but also to relieve any apprehension employees may have about the coming changes in work arrangements. BCBSMA used recorded videos that were posted to the company's intranet site.

"Over time, it was a natural progression," Kelly said. "People getting used to it, leaders seeing the benefits. Initially, people were afraid that they were out of sight, out of mind. They were afraid they would be the first ones to be laid off if there was a restructuring or that they wouldn't get promoted. Employees then started to notice that e-workers were getting promoted and leaders saw that e-workers were productive. We were then able to gain the confidence of the business leaders. We were getting lots of positive feedback. We would then use this in quarterly review meetings and continue sharing success stories."

Engaging the Right People—Constituents and Stakeholders

In his international bestseller, *Leading Change*, former Harvard Business School professor and management guru, John Kotter, stated that 75 percent of a company's management needs to "buy into" the proposed organizational change for any change effort to be successful.[1] This is more than just approval; it is visible support from key leaders. After identifying the behaviors you need to change, identifying the key stakeholder to evangelize the change is the next step. Keep in mind that the most influential people in the organization may not be just the heads of the hierarchy. Influence comes from a number of sources based on status, tenure, or expertise.

Before targeting specific individuals, start with a broad view of the organization. Identify and label key groups of people, or "constituents" who will be impacted. These groups can then be analyzed in terms of their relative influence or involvement with the implementation. Examine which groups may support or resist compared to others. Additionally, understand where the groups reside in the organization, and their relative weight or size to others. This high-level view can then be used to create a more detailed view or stakeholder analysis.

A stakeholder is any individual who can have a significant impact on or can be significantly impacted by the effort. Some may argue that a stakeholder could also be a group, department, or function. However, we recommend identifying the broad groups as your constituents and the head of that organization, or at least a key influential member of that group, as your targeted stakeholder. With these stakeholders pinpointed, you can conduct a thorough analysis. Stakeholder analysis is a process designed to align the political aspects of the organization to the needs and goals of the program.

Stakeholder analysis is typically conducted for any large-scale project or initiative, but it is particularly important to Workshift. As research has shown, the historical barriers to workplace change are management resistance and organizational culture.[2] A stakeholder analysis can help overcome these challenges by forcing the implementation team to identify all the potential parties and individuals who can positively or negatively influence the initiative and then develop strategies to align those stakeholders.

Table 5.1 Sample stakeholder analysis template

Stakeholder name & department	*Current position*	*Issues or reasons for current position*	*Needed position*	*Action plan or mitigation strategy*
Jane Doe, SVP of HR	**Support**	• Very supportive; program will likely help drive HR metrics of talent acquisition costs, retention, & employee satisfaction • SVP has created similar policies in previous companies	**Support**	• No action necessary, keep SVP informed & engaged • Can leverage to help influence other senior leaders
Mary Chen, CFO	**Neutral**	• Has not been engaged & has not reacted to business case that was developed	**Support**	• Need one-on-one conversation to cover the financials in the business case • Request for financial analyst to be part of the core team to review all figures & report back to CFO
John Smith, VP of operations	**Neutral**	• Sees the benefit to employee productivity & reduced travel costs, but is concerned about the culture change & how mid-level managers will react	**Neutral**	• Help develop specific communication & training plan for ops. dept. & have VP approve • Request a small team from ops. to go through pilot as proof of concept
Scott Jones, CIO	**Resist**	• Views this as a huge burden that IT staff will have to support • Very concerned about security, BYOD policies, & assets in the home office • Concerned about impact on IT budget	**Support**	• Need to provide CIO with detailed analysis around security concerns • Engage with asset management to discuss requirement needs • Once CFO is onboard, hold joint discussion on budget

Once the stakeholders are identified, the team can classify the stakeholders as resistant, supportive, or neutral in regard to the implementation. If the stakeholder is resistant, it's important for the team to uncover the specific reasons or issues that explain the stakeholder's position. Then, the program team can determine where they need the stakeholder to be. For example, not every stakeholder needs to support the initiative. Some may need to simply move from resistant to neutral so the stakeholder does not openly impede progress. This step will help the team prioritize, determining where to focus their communication and change management efforts. Lastly, for the identified stakeholders the team needs to align, the team can define the specific strategies to employ to get them onboard. These strategies are then translated into actions and can be added to the overall plan (see table 5.1 for a sample stakeholder analysis template). Successful implementations depend on managing a number of stakeholders. Getting them aligned prior to launch and keeping them onboard throughout the implementation is vital.

Leveraging the Champions

One of the key reasons for success at ATB Investor Services is the executive sponsorship for the program.

"Our President is a huge advocate, and pioneer around working from anywhere. Without that support, you won't be successful. You need someone to model the way," said Wright-Schwietz. "All of our executive and senior managers are very supportive and see that companies are moving away from the traditional workplace model and embracing Workshift."

In previous chapters we reiterated the importance of establishing an executive sponsor or champion from the beginning. However, sponsorship goes way beyond one individual when it comes to driving transformational change through the entire organization. The executive sponsor or top-level champion is a necessity, but the program team must create a number of champions at all levels and in various parts of the organization. Collectively, these champions can mobilize the employee population. A study by McKinsey & Company of 40 company-wide change efforts in organizations across a variety of industries highlighted the importance of engaging various levels of the organization. Interestingly, their findings pointed out that one level of the organization did not matter more than another. Companies had a better chance of success if one level of the organization, whether it was executives, middle management, or frontline employees, was fully onboard, but no level was more important than the others. Unsurprisingly, the most successful companies studied were aligned at all levels within the organization from senior management down to employees. The ROI for initiatives launched within these successful companies achieved far more, almost 150 percent, than initial expectations.[3]

Furthermore, employee engagement and allowing employees to take initiatives to help drive the change ultimately creates success, more than the acts of an individual. Research backs up this claim, demonstrating that when leaders provide frontline employees a sense of ownership, change efforts can have a 70 percent success rate. This, coupled with employees using their own initiatives to help transform the organization, can increase success rates to almost 80 percent.[4]

The question becomes: How does the program team create champions, ownership, engagement, and overcome resistance? Understanding and working with stakeholders or stakeholder groups, is a prime opportunity to leverage or create relationships that will accomplish this task. No doubt the team, and even the champions, is bound to encounter resistance. However, there are usually some common scenarios when it comes to resistance and some common ways to use the champion to help turn things in your favor.

The first common scenario is the easiest to solve. You and the stakeholder, or stakeholders, resisting adoption both report to the champion. The stakeholders push back because they don't report to you and there are no consequences for not cooperating with your effort. The answer to this problem may appear a little obvious. The champion needs to be more direct with the other members of the team who are not following through. However, keep in mind that this is not schoolyard tattling to the person in charge. That will only deepen the divide and cause some passive aggressive behavior among the stakeholders. Keep your champion informed on the progress of the entire organization and ask for some airtime during team meetings, management reviews, or all-employee meetings. Additionally, ensure the champion is publicly advocating the change and rewarding those that are making progress.

In the second scenario, the stakeholder does not report directly to the champion. The person or group you are trying to influence has a completely different reporting structure, and again, there are no consequences for noncompliance. In this situation you'll have to rely more on your marketing and selling skills. A network of supporting sponsors in the organization you are trying to influence can also help, especially if you target both senior and middle management. However, you may need different approaches for both groups. The business case, especially the what's-in-it-for-them pitch, will have to be compelling to their specific needs. Also, you need to clearly outline the risk if they do nothing and maintain the status quo.

The third, and unfortunately very common, scenario is to encounter stakeholder groups that ignore requests or mandates for adoption because local management is dictating otherwise. In other words, proximity trumps seniority and people will follow the direction of their immediate supervisors. Senior management may be supportive, or at least provide public lip service, but middle managers aren't buying it. In this case, a little peer pressure can help. Running a pilot in that group or department to demonstrate how it will work and the practical results it can achieve can help create allies within the organization and gradually expand the program. Good individual and organizational performance metrics are vital in this scenario and should help drive the business case by providing evidence of the benefits. Also, ensure senior management is not just providing vocal support but setting the right example themselves.

The above scenarios are not to suggest that you will always encounter resistance from leaders when implementing. Keep in mind that you may have many early adopters or at least strong supporters of the program. You can leverage these leaders, wherever they are in the organization, and turn them into advocates and evangelists. For Allison Comeau, head of ATB Investor Services business transformation team, adopting a flexible work environment with her employees was a no-brainer. A champion of the company's Workplace 2.0, Allison said her ten employees were dispersed across the city and each found they spent many hours a week commuting.

"The traffic in Calgary is brutal," she said. "And from our perspective, it's a huge time waster. The two hours a day my employees are sitting in traffic, going to and from the office, they could be productive."

Now, none of her employees have dedicated office space in the downtown building. Rather, they can book available space ahead of time or borrow a conference room.

Aligning Policies, Practices, Rewards, and Consequences

Many organizations do an outstanding job generating visible support, but then accidentally derail their own efforts. Leaders have to be careful to consider the things in the organization that are countering any behaviors they are trying to encourage. A variety of anecdotes illustrate this common mistake, such as the company we knew that purchased expensive video conferencing systems and wanted employees to start using it. However, the company had a very open travel policy, allowing employees to travel across the country for whatever need, even if it was only for a one-hour meeting. Why would employees flock to use video conferencing when they could always go and meet in person? Furthermore, how would the company ever achieve the financial benefits presented in the business case if there was no impact on travel expenses? A policy change was needed to help encourage the desired behavior. The company could have developed a policy or guidelines restricting travel, which would force employees to find alternative means to communicate rather than face-to-face.

Note that policy changes may not be all that is necessary to ensure a successful launch. Process and technology factors may also unknowingly hinder efforts. One bank we knew implemented a work-at-home policy, but gave no consideration beforehand to their internal work processes. For a bank loan to be approved, over a half dozen physical signatures were needed on various documents. Employees found themselves continually coming back into the office because no one had changed the process of how loans were processed or investigated other potential solutions, such as using electronic signatures. In another case, a company wanted to leverage more of the knowledge base of its employees through social media. As management recommended various social media platforms, IT leaders were coincidentally announcing security concerns over third-party software and social media. In both cases, planners failed to identify all the factors that would affect adoption.

Lastly, we would be remiss if we didn't mention the power of positive and negative reinforcement on changing behavior. We are not necessarily talking about traditional methods of rewards and punishments, but the more creative measures some leaders have taken to encourage the right behaviors. For example, positive reinforcement comes in many forms. From the organizations we've reviewed, many used public recognition to not only highlight best practices but single out individuals, teams, or departments that exhibit desired traits. Additionally, participation metrics in some organizations are used as a means of positive reinforcement. Metrics may be reported for each internal department, reviewed by senior management, and available to all employees. The competitive nature within the organization can encourage increased participation. Leaders can also employ other simple techniques to encourage adoption, such as devoting a portion of their staff or all-employee meetings to the initiative and recognizing those who are leading the way.

The ultimate form of positive reinforcement for employees could be in terms of career progression. Many employees express apprehension to participate for a variety of reasons. One of their biggest fears is that their advancement to higher positions will be impeded by working virtually. Recognizing this, leaders can ensure that promotions or rotational opportunities are equally available between those who work in the traditional workspace and those who do not. Even a perceived bias can greatly hinder adoption and leaders must ensure the playing field is level for all employees.

Conversely, leaders must also carefully consider repercussions for noncompliance with stated objectives. What should leaders do when there is a particular team or department that has low or no participation? Working directly with leaders in those areas can help uncover the root causes of whether the lack of participation is due to perception issues or is openly discouraged by local management. Often, direct attention from senior leaders is all that is necessary to encourage laggards.

Technology as a Creative Catalyst

Given that Workshift depends on technology, it seems intuitive that organizations would leverage various collaborative tools and technologies to engage employees and facilitate change. Many organizations that we spoke with have an intranet or internal publication, like an e-newsletter, to announce and publicize the program or share success stories and best practices. Additionally, most organizations are already using their intranet to deliver web-based training, both live and self-paced. Although these methods are adequate to broadcast general information, there are far more options available to leaders trying to mobilize the employee population. For example, social networking sites, video, blogs, wikis, and discussion boards are just a few options that are readily available for most organizations.

The USDA effectively uses YouTube to share success stories. The agency allows employees to tell their personal stories by creating and posting YouTube videos that can be viewed by anyone. The success stories or "day-in-the-life" testimonials create an opportunity for early adopters to be recognized among their peers and provide employees outside the telework program team with a window into the lives of virtual employees. Other federal agencies and private-sector companies also share videos in similar ways.

Through our research we also came into contact with companies trying to use blogs and discussion boards to connect employees. Senior management wasn't trying to disseminate information; rather, employees were directly accessing the knowledge and lessons learned from other employees. In some cases, employees were creating discussions in real time to solve IT-related problems, such as when an employee was having trouble setting up a new IP phone, instead of contacting their local IT help desk for support. We have no empirical data to validate this claim, but employees forming their own type of support groups seemed to accelerate adoption because employees were engaged, were aware that many others were already doing it, or were confident they had others to turn to when help was needed.

While discussion boards and blogs were more frequently used, we did find organizations just starting to leverage internal social networking sites to engage employees. Employees could identify self-proclaimed experts across the company in any location and connect with those experts to use as resources. The ability to instantaneously tap into a large pool of experts promises to help accelerate adoption as well as allow virtual employees to collaborate better.

Although we didn't find any examples of gamification being used to increase adoption, we do expect this trend to impact Workshift in the near future. Many frequent travelers are used to reward points and achieving a certain status or ranking within an airline program. This same "game" concept may soon be applied to encourage virtual working. For example, to encourage participation, individuals or teams could earn points that would elevate themselves to a designated virtual status. Or, internal telework experts could earn credits or points based on the quantity or quality of information they provide to other employees. However leaders choose to leverage this concept, gamification may help many organizations in the future to produce desired behaviors and break through resistance.

Gamification: Using game elements and game design in non-game contexts

Framing Change the Right Way

Even with the right executive stakeholder support, policy alignment, and reward structure, some organizations may still run into employee or manager resistance. Some of this resistance can be explained by the behavioral economic theory known as Prospect Theory. This theory tries to explain how people choose between different alternatives that involve some level of risk. Brittany Martin of the University of Calgary directly links Prospect Theory and organizational adoption of telework programs. According to Martin, decisions are made subconsciously based on a frame of reference that centers on an inferred or perceived reference point. Martin points out that people want to avoid loss more than avoiding risk when making a decision. However, people will seek risk to avoid losing altogether.[5]

In other words, employees evaluate whether or not to participate in a telework or similar program based on their reference point. For many employees, that reference point is the traditional work arrangement and office setting. When presenting Workshift to employees, employees and managers may perceive risk in various ways, such as negative impacts on future career progression, decreased productivity, lack of collaboration, or less employee engagement. Yet, the change, and perceived risks, may be tolerable if *not* changing results in unacceptable loss (e.g., a manager would lose an employee who is relocating if he or she was not allowed to work remotely).

Given that managerial perception is one of the top barriers cited in telework adoption, Martin's doctoral research examined whether framing can be used strategically to influence a change in mind. She found that changing the frame of reference can shift managerial mind-sets about telework. In a lab study of 146 business students and 84 senior managers, findings revealed that a "deeply embedded bias for traditional work acts as a barrier to telework adoption."[6] Managers resist telework by subconsciously dismissing it as something new and perceive it as too different or unfamiliar from what they know. However, her findings also identify and test specific changes to the decision frame that, in turn, change minds.

Designing a frame of reference that can influence a shift in preferences is not as simple as it sounds. The trick is in embedding a reference point explicitly enough "to elicit cognitive processes that either draw upon or over-rule the status quo bias in such a way that telework is perceived as a gain, or at least a risk worth taking."[7] It's important to note that such a frame is only meant to influence a quick decision based on limited information and could be overruled with cognitive effort, awareness of the frame, or portfolio analysis. However, given the assumption that low organizational adoption is based on a quick dismissal owing to a bias for traditional work, it makes sense to intervene by explicitly reframing the decision in a way that is more favorable. Specifically, Martin identifies three frames that showed a shift in preferences by approximately 20 percent.[8]

First, Martin recommends framing Workshift as the status quo. If everyone in the company or in the industry is doing it, then it will not necessarily be perceived as something new. The program team may have already benchmarked other companies or found pockets of employees in the company who are informally or formally working virtually to build the business case. This information can also be leveraged as part of the communication strategy to the broader organization to help managers recognize its commonality or how pervasive it is.

Second, Workshift can be framed similar to traditional work. It may be similar to existing flexible work or telework options and therefore be familiar to managers. This may help explain the success of some organizations using an au naturel approach. Considering that working virtually is a natural way for these organizations to do business, any expansion of the program is quickly integrated into overall work practices. However, with many of the organizations we interviewed it seemed common practice to brand the workplace change. Although this internal marketing campaign appeared to generate excitement within the organization, it can be a double-edged sword. Planners should be aware that if the change is perceived as too radical, dramatic, or unfamiliar, it may create apprehension and resistance. However planners decide to brand their program, they should be careful on how it is articulated to managers and employees so as to not unintentionally slow adoption.

Lastly, it can be framed as having advantages not available to traditional workers. For example, benefits of reducing CRE, acquiring talent in lower cost areas, allowing employees to work close to a client site, or working across multiple time zones may only be feasible if the organization adopts alternative means of working. This frame confirms what many planners have learned through trial and error: One of the biggest influencers to organizational change is the tangible results of the program, especially the results that can only be achieved through Workshift. When leaders see the ROI and can feel the impact, momentum will quickly build. Again, ATB is an example of how results translate into continued adoption and success. When the company piloted the program, 30 participated out of the 350 employees in Investor Services. An additional 130 began the transition soon after the pilot. For 2013, it is expected that another 150 will adopt their Workplace 2.0 program. The large jumps in participation can be traced back to the benefits the company is realizing.

Mike Frederick claimed the money saved by moving employees out of the office is significant. ATB Investor Services has saved more than $600,000 in leasing costs in Calgary and Edmonton alone in the first year of Workplace 2.0 and expects those savings to continue to grow. As an example, the company is saving on parking costs—Frederick had a downtown parking space that was costing $500 per month. Now, there are fewer parking spots and employees can book the space ahead of time, similar to office space. And by not having employees at their desks eight hours a day, five days a week, the company is reducing its office footprint and saving money on utilities as well. But for ATB, the benefits go beyond the financials and ties back to their original business case of increasing retention and employee satisfaction.

"But by far the biggest driver for us has been employee engagement," Frederick said. "Calgary is a very competitive market for employees and flexibility is a big part of it. We're committed to employee development and retention."

Putting It All Together

It is important to remember that changing organizational behavior is a continuous activity and is not something done just prior to launch. Although we present the Engage stage as a separate and distinct phase, the reality is that it is often woven into the entire lifecycle. It may be good practice for leaders to pause after their detailed plan is developed to ensure change management activities are aligned to the strategy or to ensure they have created mitigation plans for the anticipated resistance from certain employee segments. However, engaging leaders and employees is never a one-time activity, nor does it stop when the program is launched. Leaders need to constantly revisit their engagement plan, make revisions, and continue to execute to increase chances of success. Even well after the program is launched and early signs of success can be measured, the activities from the Engage stage must continue (see table 5.2) to ensure the program doesn't plateau and the organization can realize all the benefits.

Table 5.2 Engage activities

	Investigate	*Discover*	*Design*	*Engage*	*Launch & scale*	*Measure*	*Leverage*
Executive sponsors & stakeholders	• Identify & engage exec sponsor • Create value proposition	• Create & present business case	• Exec sponsor approve implementation plan	• Stakeholder analysis • Socialize business case and plan	• Confirm sponsors & stakeholders communicating to employees	• Assess sponsor & stakeholder alignment & effectiveness	• Confirm desired behaviors are in place
Behavior changes		• Complete organizational assessment	• Determine behavior changes & build into plan	• Determine rewards, recognition, & consequences	• Ensure feedback loops are in place to monitor behaviors	• Determine if desired behaviors are being modeled	• Reevaluate behaviors needed for sustained change
Communication	• Create elevator pitch	• Determine constituent groups & needs	• Create communication strategy & plan	• Execute communication plan • Publicize pilot success	• Publish success stories & quick wins • Iterative communication	• Assess communication plan effectiveness	• Revise comms plan based on launch results
Metrics	• Determine high-level success metrics	• Refine success metrics	• Determine pilot metrics • Assess pilot	• Determine employee engagement metrics	• Collect data & feedback • Identify quick wins	• Evaluate change management efforts	• Reassess metrics & determine add'l requirements
Training		• Determine initial needs	• Create training plan	• Execute training	• Execute training • Refine training based on feedback	• Evaluate training results • Determine additional training needs	• Execute add'l training as needed
Risk mitigation	• Address exec sponsor concerns	• Identify risks from org. assessment	• Develop mitigation plans • Refine plans based on pilot results	• Reassess risks & mitigation plans	• Execute risk mitigation plan	• Evaluate risk mitigation plans & determine additional actions needed	• Evaluate risk mitigation plans & determine add'l actions needed

Stage 4: Engage—Summary

Key activities in this phase are:

- Consensus building and communication
- Addressing existing limitations of organization culture and management behavior that may inhibit the adoption of Workshift
- Storytelling—why Workshifting is great for the company, employees, and community
- Myth-busting

Deliverables:

- Communication plan
- Stakeholder analysis
- Change acceptance plan
- Success stories or case studies

Key risks:

- Nobody signs up (this is a symptom of something besides desire)
- Certain managers block participation, knowingly and/or unknowingly
- Senior leaders are not giving enough attention or airtime to the program

CHAPTER 6

Launch

Launching a product is similar to launching a rocket—you have to break the tremendous inertia that is holding the body at rest.

—Neale Martin

Through our research for this book, we learned that many organizations have teleworkers, but few designed and followed a plan to implement a formal Workshift program. We also learned that organizations, especially more established companies that informally allow telework or enable small programs to organically grow into larger ones without following a defined plan, tend to miss opportunities to realize the widely recognized and promoted benefits of telework. Because of this, we devote this entire chapter to an illustration based on what one financial services company did to engage in a substantive process to launch a formal program. To explain the many factors and details that contribute to a successful implementation, we have added recommendations for an enterprise-wide launch and subsequent scaling of a Workshift program.

We recognize that every organization is unique and not all organizations will require the same level of rigor based on size, organizational culture, infrastructure, experience, and goals or business outcomes expected. However, the approach and techniques recommended in this chapter may serve as guideposts for program teams. What follows is an in-depth view of the steps needed to assess and discover an organization's as-is state and readiness for evolving an informal telework program to a more formal program that illustrates steps we outlined in the preceding stages: Investigate, Discover, and Engage. Design elements of a more formalized program, including the development of policies, procedures, training, and a pilot program as identified in chapter 4, are described in detail. Examples of the important role communications and engagement play in fertilizing the ground for ensuring a successful Launch are pinpointed. We take what we have anchored in previous chapters to a fully dimensional view of a planning and execution process that will create a way forward for launching an expanded, and a more formalized, program. Practical examples are included throughout this chapter that can be tailored and replicated in any organization preparing to launch a pilot program, and useful lessons learned are reflected throughout many elements of the iterative process and approach.

Where Did Everybody Go?

Most organizations have a certain number of employees who are engaged in a form or frequency of off-site work. Casual walks through the office may reveal office vacancies. Many employees may already be working outside of the office even if these employees don't travel frequently. You may ask: Why are we still paying for more space than we seem to need?

With this initial question in mind, your organization may kick off the Investigate stage. A cross-functional team consisting of members from risk management, information security, HR, legal compliance, IT, and corporate real estate may start to formulate a value proposition. With initial support from executive sponsors, the team can move into the Discover stage and gather the necessary data to fully develop a business case. In addition to assessing organizational culture, IT infrastructure, and spacing needs, the team should gather information on the current state of telework to alternative work arrangements in the organization. For example, the team should study historical information about how alternative work arrangements/telework evolved at the firm, the current state and existing participation rates, and program cost and organization cost savings analysis.

Alternative work practices may have evolved at the firm for a variety of reasons to address different individual and business needs.

It is important to document this information as a baseline for validating the need to continue to provide these work arrangement options for managers and employees. Programs may evolve over time based on special situations. For example, part-time telecommuting agreements may be more common than full-time telework arrangements and each department may handle telework arrangements differently. The timeline of the Workshift evolution at the firm may indicate that it is more commonplace with the use of portable technology, laptops, and smartphones. Alternative work arrangements may be driven mainly by employees seeking to be at home or to avoid commuting—not driven by space considerations or other company concerns.

The program team should look at existing participation rates and whether enterprise-wide formal written policies exist. Commonly, we find that many employees have some form of telework or flexible work agreement in place, but agreements are unwritten or used inconsistently. If available, the team can leverage any centralized database or software tracking system that may already be in use to capture and report data on the population of teleworkers and validate the exact number of executed telecommuting agreements.

To view the organizational cost savings analysis of telework, the team should establish a baseline for the costs referenced in their business case by assembling a number of data points: current real estate cost (rent and occupancy costs per rentable square foot) for each of their main corporate offices and the daily cost of hoteling space used by teleworkers enrolled in the program (if hoteling or workspace sharing practices are in use).

Arriving at these costs will require the team to revisit the telework proposal that documents how departments with telecommuters who gave up permanent seat assignments would be relieved of their rent and occupancy charge-back costs associated with the released space. In these cases, a manager and an employee should have the option of either cube sharing with an associate within their business unit at no additional rent and occupancy cost to the business unit, or an employee could reserve a seat from the telecommuter seat pool on-site. A business unit would still be responsible for the cost associated with the use of a seat in the shared pool, so a daily cost could be calculated, if needed, of these shared seats based on current rent and occupancy rates at each of their large locations.

Establishing a consistent, enterprise-wide telework policy

With the completion of the Discover phase, the team could start planning for an enterprise-wide Workshift policy as part of the Design stage. While some type of policy may govern all of the existing work arrangements within departments, there needs to be consistency from one department to another. Therefore, we suggest an enterprise-wide policy that addresses the following considerations:

- A definition of the firm's alternative workplace approach as a program designed to better match employees to work arrangements that best suit their role, job function, work style, and personality traits. A distinction between formal, manager-approved work-from-home arrangements, flexible work options, and/or part-time telecommuting.
- A consistent process for approving alternative work agreements. In addition to the direct manager's approval, the department's senior executive and HR manager should review the agreement. Any employees with federal licenses and registrations should be required to have their work-from-home agreement approved by a compliance team.
- A consistent approach regardless of where employees worked. Workshifting employees would be subject to all corporate policies in the same manner as if they were working on-site.
- A role and business need focus. Approval to participate in the program needs to be role-focused, and should be initiated to meet business needs rather than focus exclusively on personal or individualized needs of employees.

Proposed Standardized Operational Procedures for the Program

We have found that variability often exists in the approach each business takes to identify employees suitable for participation in a Workshift arrangement and the process of executing their work arrangement agreement. As a result, the following guidelines are

Table 6.1 Standard enrollment guidelines

1	Approval process should be consistent and include the execution of a formal agreement between the employee and manager. Thee executed agreement should be held and managed by human resources.
2	Work arrangement should be subject to a quarterly review by the manager.
3	Telework arrangements may be modified at any time based on the business needs of the organization. Employees should be given a 30 day notice in advance of the termination of a telework agreement.
4	Employees should be required to meet several eligibility requirements in order to participate in the program, including 6 months full-time tenure and a level of "satisfactory" or higher on their most recent performance review.
5	Business units and human resources should establish a standard set of ineligibility factors which may include such items as information security, on site work or staff support duties, specific management responsibilities, information technology limitations, supervision requirements mandated by federal regulatory agencies and established face-to-face client meeting requirements.
6	Teleworkers must be provided with the training and equipment necessary to maintain information security per corporate policies.
7	The program team and human resources should establish organization-wide guidelines for work schedule, work hours, overtime eligibility standards and timekeeping requirements.

recommended to facilitate a standardized enrollment and work arrangement management process (table 6.1):

Home Office Provisioning and Rules

Many organizations overlook the importance of creating guidelines for the home office workspace. Rather than overreaching by providing too many requirements, a few fundamental points should be emphasized: The organization may provide remote or home-based employees with such equipment as a laptop, multifunctional printer, shredder, and an ergonomic chair. Home office provisioning should be based on whether an employee releases their assigned workspace on-site or continues to work on-site in a shared space. If an employee has no assigned workspace on-site and they were working primarily from home, then they should be provisioned accordingly. Likewise, employees who still have a shared space on-site and spend less time at home may require less equipment and supplies for their home office. Employees should be prohibited from doing company work on non-company equipment. Additionally, employees should not be allowed to host in-person business meetings in their homes and employees should have all work mail delivered to a company location, if possible, where it will be opened and stored until the employee comes on-site to retrieve it or it is forwarded to them.

Guidelines for Managing Teleworkers

Many managers may have little or no experience managing employees at a distance and need guidelines that establish a framework for managing virtual employees. Specific guidance for enabling managers to succeed should include:

- Providing managers with a single source of reference for all corporate policies that impact teleworkers and their managers, such as the code of business conduct, electronic communication policy, and information security policy.
- Providing managers training on how to effectively supervise employee's handling of confidential information.
- Encouraging managers to establish workplace guidelines including work hours and requirements of on-site office time.
- Discussing general principles on managing employees from a distance, including:
    - Focussing on deliverables and results, not on the amount of time spent on tasks.
    - Establishing requirements for communicating output through either daily or weekly work logs.
    - Overtime eligible employees may be required to carefully track time and expenses.
    - Meeting with employees to regularly review and discuss timesheets and/or work logs.
    - Empowering and trusting telecommuters to balance priorities and apply the right processes, procedures, and efficiencies consistent with guidelines and mature judgment.
- Providing a general outline of training requirements for managers and their employees.

In the Design stage we addressed the importance of training. Below we outline specific goals of both manager and employee training used by some companies (tables 6.2 and 6.3).

Table 6.2 Manager training objectives

1	Assist managers in overcoming fears about loss of control or decrease in their authority.
2	Enable managers to better identify telework-suitable job functions and select suitable candidates for telework.
3	Provide managers with tools to assist in the process of managing varied work schedules across multiple sites.
4	Establish open communications between physically separated employees, including those teleworking as well as those working on site in different locations.
5	Provide timely feedback to telecommuters using all available methods of communication, including email, voice, instant messaging (if available) and regularly scheduled face-to-face meetings.

Table 6.3 Employee training objectives

1	Overcome the fear of unfair performance evaluation and harm to career associated with the perception of working off-site as being "out of sight, out of mind."
2	Logistics planning, ensuring one's home office configured effectively and has all of the necessary resources and materials.
3	Skills to enable employees to manage time effectively and maintain high levels of productivity while working remotely.
4	Strategies for keeping open lines of communication with the supervisors and co-workers.
5	Resources and activities to foster and improve remote collaboration.
6	Techniques to help address common work-at-home issues (proper use of workspace, preparing family, etc.)

Next Steps and Program Implementation Timeline

Based on the data collected from a number of organizations and research on industry best practices, we offer a number of suggestions for next steps in the implementation process (table 6.4).

Table 6.4 Implementation recommendations

1	Establish a steering committee comprised of cross-functional, director-level leadership to design and implement a pilot of the organization's ability to support telework in a standardized fashion enterprise-wide.
2	Create consistent employee telework agreement, policy and standard operating procedure documents in conjunction with applicable business area leadership.
3	Obtain approvals of program documents and processes as official corporate policy.
4	Design pilot that tests the organizations ability to successfully support teleworkers and managers while still meeting the needs of the business.
5	Develop telecommuting training programs for employees and managers to enable them to be effective working, communicating and managing from a distance.
6	Develop a timeline and establish goals for the program's design, pilot, implementation and evaluation.

Can We Do This?

Testing the organization's ability to support a formal, enterprise-wide Workshift program is the first step in the launch process. A well-designed pilot enables the program manager to determine whether the organization has the processes, resources, and infrastructure in place to kick off the program. Depending on the type of activities that have occurred prior to the launch decision, different organizations have used different methods to determine how to pilot their program and test launch readiness.

Based on our experience, there are three factors to assess during the pilot. First, determine if the program model is effective for all employee and manager roles in the company. Telework arrangements may not be suited for every type of employee or work role, and these work styles could vary drastically within an organization. A pilot may include a representative sample comprised of employees working in every different business unit and in as many different work roles as possible. The program team should select work roles that may be best suited to remote work.

Next, the program team needs to understand whether employees are satisfied with the organization's ability to support them while they work remotely. During the pilot, a simple method can be used to determine whether employees are satisfied with the participation in the program. Just ask them! A short time into the pilot a simplified survey can be distributed, asking a few questions of each participant, such as: "Are you satisfied with your participation in the Workshift pilot?" Using a five-point Likert scale, responses can be tabulated with a goal of having a target percent or more of the employees responding "satisfied" or "very satisfied" with the program. In later pilot phases and on into Launch, more detailed instruments can be developed to assess both employee and manager satisfaction with the program, as well as an assessment of other factors, including equipment provisioning and technical support.

In addition to the quantitative question on satisfaction, feedback can be gathered on all other aspects of the program. However, we caution program teams to not let the list of questions grow to an unwieldy size. Instead of sending pilot participants a huge survey of questions, just a few comment fields that prompt participants to provide open-ended answers on a variety of topics should suffice. The information gleaned from the program participants is invaluable for the design of the program launch.

Lastly, the team should know if employees continue to work remotely after they enrolled in the program. Responding to a survey is not sufficient to gauge program success effectively. Tracking employee retention in the program provides an added dimension to determine program efficacy. Program retention can be calculated by tabulating the gross number of people who leave the program regardless of the reason. (Ensure to document the reason for withdrawing from the program.) The retention rate can be then be compared to the participation goal established for the program.

As a final note, the program team may consider excluding current teleworkers from participating in the study. Employees currently engaged in a telework or flexible work agreement, "legacy telecommuters," may be excluded from eligibility to participate in the pilot because the pilot's success is on converting traditional office-bound workers to teleworkers, remote, or mobile workers. Measuring employees already teleworking or working remotely will skew results. While legacy teleworkers can be folded into the formal program at a later date, there is little value in testing new processes or procedures on this cohort during the pilot.

Quantifying and Leveraging Lessons Learned

We believe the planning for a pilot is critical to the success of a program launch. If an organization elects to formalize a legacy approach to supporting employees rather than piloting or testing their ability to support a program, an important opportunity is missed to gather data necessary to make informed decisions on the design of the launch. We recommend designing a pilot assessment that captures more data, both in-flight and at the conclusion of the pilot. To start with, the program team can ask the following key questions to get a high-level understanding of the pilot impact and recommendations going forward:

1. *Was there a well-defined plan for the pilot?* Were new processes, performance metrics, goals, or expectations tested, or was the intent to replicate the same things done in the past, but now with a larger number of participants? The plan should include

expectations for results and a method for measuring, both quantitatively and qualitatively, whether the pilot failed to meet, met, or exceeded expectations.

2. *What met or exceeded expectations?* The value of the pilot will seem to be a "no-brainer" for program leaders, participants, and advocates, but it's important to capture data on the best components of the pilot to ensure these aspects carry forward through the launch. These results will also serve as talking points with those hesitant or concerned about participating in the program as it scales.
3. *What could we have done better?* The list of challenges to the success or effectiveness of the program will become the primary task list for program launch. Whether they are casual observations or actual process issues, each opportunity for change or improvement should be documented, evaluated, and migrated to the launch plan.
4. *Did we have the right stakeholders defined?* Typically, one's assumptions regarding the extent of the impact of telework on an organization are incorrect or incomplete. When the pilot plan was designed, these assumptions led to decisions on the composition of the pilot team and the involvement of other stakeholders in the program. Completion of the pilot is a good time to reevaluate the team to ensure all necessary stakeholders were engaged.
5. *Were roles and responsibilities clear?* For many organizations, no one on the pilot or launch team has testing or implementation of Workshift listed in their job description. It's important to determine if the tasks associated with program implementation and management were properly assigned, whether the right people were on the implementation team, and if the team was the right size. It's a good opportunity to identify data points necessary to validate the business case and determine if more resources are needed to support the program when it launches.

With information captured on overall lessons learned, the team can begin to dive a little deeper into specific aspects of the pilot.

1. *Were the goals of the pilot clear?* Many of the issues that arise are rooted in communication problems, and common

communication problems associated with any change management program is a lack of clarity, consistency, and completeness in the communication of program goals. Successfully communicating the program goals to stakeholders, participants, and the entire organization is a key ingredient to a successful pilot.

2. *What communication methods worked best? Least?* Common forms of business communication (e.g., mass email blasts, digital newsletters, company intranet site, etc.) as well as social media may be used.
3. *Were the right audiences communicated to?* Early in the launch process, communication is usually focused on two groups: program participants and managers. Messaging can provide information related to program issues and progress made toward realizing program goals. As the program matures, program leaders also need to provide employees not involved in the program with information about the company's Workshift community. Nonparticipating employees will interact with program participants as the program grows.

In addition to understanding the communication methods and processes, the team also needs to address issues around finance and costs.

1. *Was the program's financial data presented effectively?* Every organization is driven by different financial data points. One organization's key metric may be maximizing the headcount number supported by a given facility, and another may be driven by the cost of rent and occupancy per person. While both organizations have the same desire to reduce costs and increase utilization, they approach delivery of information from a different angle. It's important to make sure the program data is captured and reported using the organization's vocabulary of value.
2. *Were financial objectives and cost targets met?* It can be difficult to successfully identify and report ROI and other financial data with the small sample size of the pilot. If, however, it is a component of the pilot plan, it must be addressed in data collection and program performance reports.

Designing the Launch Pad

Although each organization is different and their culture is unique, our review of successful programs shows several factors are key to successful transition from pilot to organization-wide launch.

Enrollment Process

The primary component of a successful launch is having a consistent process to move employees through the enrollment process from initial interest through work agreement approval. Although each business unit may have different operational processes and

Table 6.5 Nine step enrollment process

1	Program Overview	Employees and managers interested in participating completed an overview course that provided a consistent source of information about the program.
2	Suitability Assessment	Employees answered questioned on a web-based survey designed to capture data necessary for their managers to better understand the work arrangement best suited for the employee.
3	Manager/Employee Meeting	The manager and employee met to review the Suitability Assessment results and discuss the new work arrangement.
4	Pre-Change Survey	Participants completed a 60 question survey designed to collect baseline data necessary to measure program efficacy and employee satisfaction with the enrollment process.
5	Training	Employees completed a three-module course on program information, info security, and law/compliance.
6	Policy Review	Employees acknowledged that they have read the company's telecommuting policy.
7	Work Agreement	Employees viewed a template of the telecommuting agreement and entered information on the proposed work schedule.
8	Approvals	Managers reviewed the agreement and either approved or returned to the employees for revision. Upon manager approval, the enrollment documents were sent to human resources and other departments for approval.
9	Transition Period	Employee begins thirty-day transition period to begin working in new work arrangement. The trial period was designed to reduce the stress of changing an employee's work arrangement overnight. For the next month, the employee could still access their workspace on site and had the opportunity to ease into new work habits.

requirements, it's important for an organization to establish a consistent process to standardize a program enrollment process. This can be summarized with the following nine-step enrollment process example (table 6.5).

Communication

While many workplace studies have shown that employees embrace the opportunity to work from home, implementation teams often encounter significant push back. Objections range from not having a suitable place to work while at home to fear that being away from the office would make remote employees more likely to lose their job in a force reduction or outsourcing scenario.

The program team can proactively disseminate information about the launch of the enterprise-wide program. The goal is to successfully address concerns and gain support for the program among employees and managers. A comprehensive communications program for potential participants, managers, and executives may include many mediums or approaches. Some best practices include:

- *Town hall meetings*: Meeting dedicated to an individual business unit. The program team can present a detailed overview of the program, and executives from the business unit, as well as HR and corporate real estate, should be on hand to lead a "no holds barred" question and answer (Q&A) session. Questions and answers generated during these sessions can be collated and published on the program's frequently asked questions web page (if used).
- *Morning coffee talks*: Town halls may intimidate some employees and many leave the meetings with important, unanswered questions. The program team can reserve space in common areas, such as the cafeteria or break room, and hold informal conversations about the program.
- *Weekly community calls*: Branding the participants in the program as being members of a "community" can help break down the walls associated with the perception that "if we work for different departments we can't share our successes or challenges of working in this new way." In addition to sending group communications to the community, the program

team can host recurring conference calls or meetings. During these meetings, program leaders can update participants on program issues, changes, and other news. The leadership team can also moderate a Q&A session to allow community members to communicate issues and share their experiences with other members of the community. The meeting can be a successful method for providing the community with a single point of contact for program information and a convenient way to share their experience with their coworkers.

Participation Suitability Assessment

While not every employee is suited for Workshift, it is often difficult to assess which employees are best or least suited for it. Managers can determine an employee's suitability for the program by assessing several key factors (table 6.6).

Table 6.6 Participation suitability assessment

Work location	What amount of an employee's work time was spent working in different types of work locations?
Communications	What amount of time was spent engaged in a variety of different forms of communication?
Group interactions	What amount of formal and informal interactions was spent with internal and external business groups?
Work activities	What work activities use various levels of focus, communication and interaction?
Specialized work resources	What location specific resources were required?
Work preferences and characteristics	What is the required, preferred use, and frequency of different workspaces?

Training

Training is one of the most important resources for virtual employees and their managers. First, the program team should establish a set of guiding assumptions. Recognize that establishing a training program, including content and delivery methodology, is a substantial task and will not happen overnight. The rollout of training needs to be staggered over a period of time. In some cases, for large organizations, it can take 18–24 months. Additionally, training needs to be sustainable and blended over several delivery media. Both employees and managers may comprise the first wave of participants. Given the various skills, background, and experiences of participating employees, participation plans should be subject to fluctuation, and the ability to test out of training should be available. There is no need to waste resources reinventing the wheel; engaging training solutions and consultants with experience in working virtually is usually recommended. Training should not be limited to employees enrolled in the program and their managers. It should include those directly affected as well as the employee population as a whole. Training should be structured to accommodate variability in the pace of learning and different learning styles. It should also allow for self-paced training and include an option for employees and managers to share best practices, feedback, and support. A key component of the training content is an understanding of how the program evolved, program objectives, and goals. The intent of the training plan is to build awareness first, then create action (skill building), followed by accountability (performance).

Using these guiding principles, a training curriculum should have the following three components:

1. *Training during enrollment*: Brief training that provides an overview of the program on-boarding process.
2. *Training on managing remotely*: Training for managers that provides guidance on how to effectively lead a remote or virtual workforce.
3. *Continuing education*: Courses designed to meet the business needs of the company (may best be delivered by a third-party vendor).

Revalidating Work Arrangements

Measuring productivity can be challenging in any conversation about the performance of employees working off-site. One of the biggest challenges associated with this issue is the idea of how to collect and use performance data outside of the HR team's clearly defined performance management processes and systems. This issue can be resolved by collecting feedback from managers about how employees are performing in the new work arrangement. Managers can meet with their employees to discuss the current work arrangement and to discuss four points regarding employee performance:

- The quality of work product;
- The quantity of work product;
- The timeliness of work product submittal; and
- Their ability to get in contact with the employee.

Tracking the resulting data and the directional trend of the data over time will enable the program team to report metrics of the key factors that are commonly associated with performance of knowledge-based workers.

Scaling the Program

The management and resource requirements for expanding a program are different from those of a program that has just started. Some ambiguity may exist in determining the exact point at which a program graduates from launching to scaling. For this reason, we define a program in the scaling phase when the program's resource requirements or delivery of value exceeds those outlined in the initial program plan or business case. For example, when the program requires dedicated staff to manage enrollment or participant support, or the space savings realized exceed expectations, the program is starting to scale.

For large enterprises, there may be concern over the cultural impact and infrastructure requirements of having large groups of people enrolling and participating all at once. A carefully managed approach to scaling the program may be necessary to successfully respond to unanticipated issues. In such cases, we recommend the concepts of lead teams and enrollment waves to manage enrollment in the program in order to scale the program in a manageable fashion.

Lead Teams

Lead teams are groups of employees within the same business unit who enroll in the program together. Executives and managers within each business unit can work together to identify groups of employees suited to and interested in enrolling in the program, and assign them to their lead team. The program team can coordinate the preparation for program enrollment, participation approval, provisioning, and training of these individuals as a group rather than as individual employees. Using this technique, the program team can efficiently provide better resources to each group and ensure that individuals in the later stages of the program implementation receive the same or better level of support as those during the pilot and launch phases.

Enrollment Waves

At the completion of the pilot, the program team should have data around the amount of time necessary for pilot participants to navigate the process, including the enrollment, approval, training, and provisioning stages. This data may be derived by analyzing data from service requests from the IT help desk, facilities service desk, and other support services. We have found that the majority of people in large organizations who require support during the enrollment process are likely to need help during the first two weeks of on-boarding into the program.

While the lead team solves the problem of efficiently preparing large numbers of people to enroll in the program, significant concerns may still exist about the organization's ability to successfully provide a large number of employees with support during this initial two-week period. The solution is often to not let employees enroll in the process at any time and instead group employees into enrollment time blocks.

Enrollment time blocks can be periods designed to incorporate a bulk of the on-boarding process of a given lead team. The process begins when the program team meets with the mangers of each lead team and asks them to reserve a slot in an enrollemnt wave. Those managers eager to enroll their teams early may be motivated to start the enrollment process or risk waiting for a later wave cycle. Once a lead team is assigned to an enrollment wave, the wave can be closed and no other employees may be enrolled in the program during that time period.

This process mutually benefits all program participants and stakeholders by enabling the support groups, including IT, HR, and corporate real estate to handle larger numbers of people in the early stages of the enrollment process, with the same level of service as the much smaller pilot group. Together, the lead team and enrollment wave approaches enable a large company to quickly and significantly scale a program enterprise-wide, without adding the risk of significant, widespread, and unintended cultural impacts or technical support consequences.

Key Factors to Successfully Launching and Scaling

Many factors, both internal and external to the organization, contribute to a successful launch. Key factors are:

- Creating and maintaining a strong advisory team
- Conducting a pilot to test the ability to provide support, equipment, and technology resources
- Managing the pace of implementation using lead teams from each business unit and assigning them to enrollment waves
- Providing multiple training/support platforms and communication channels
- Treating teleworkers as members of a community
- Working actively to assess and respond to issues

The Launch stage is the culmination of activities described in previous phases. Information gathered in the Discover stage, which is then used to craft a tailored plan in the Design stage, will ultimately lead to the successful launch and sacling of a Workshift program. As a final reminder, organizations are different and approach organizational transformation from various points in the Workshift spectrum. It is up to the program leadership to determine the best tactics and techniques based on the unique needs of the business and adapt the best practices to fit their organization.

Stage 5: Launch—Summary

Key activities in this phase are:

- Ongoing communication updates
- Including nonparticipants in feedback
- Aggregating data and presenting to key decision-makers and stakeholders on a regular basis

- Addressing concerns swiftly
- Connect the program to compelling events

Deliverables:

- Pilot results
- Training results
- Initial results of success metrics

Key risks:

- Change in leadership
- Data isn't captured adequately
- Results, successes aren't shared or encouraged widely
- Team loses steam and pilot program becomes the final step

CHAPTER 7

Measure

> The only man I know who behaves sensibly is my tailor; he takes my measurements anew each time he sees me. The rest go on with their old measurements and expect me to fit them.
>
> —George Bernard Shaw

As we studied the growing Workshift trend and how companies conducted needs analysis, and designed and implemented programs, it became clear that there were few examples of systemic approaches to determining a program's efficacy in meeting its initial goals. Nor were there many examples of how organizations gathered data to refine the program to meet the evolving needs of employees and the organization. With few exceptions, programs seemed to proclaim success if only a few qualitative measures were met, such as whether or not employees and managers participated in the program, whether the program helped mitigate stress by reducing weekly commute times, or if there was some perceived reduction in corporate space or related costs. Success needs to be measured and tracked objectively, not simply identified anecdotally. In doing so, the program is more likely to successfully integrate into the corporate culture as a key component of its workplace and human capital management strategies.

In this chapter, we explore the difference between program and organizational metrics, key metrics that capture the data necessary to determine program success and how different program phases benefit from different analyses. To provide context to this review of metrics, we offer examples of data collection and analytical approaches used by a couple of organizations as they successfully guided program evolution and maturation.

Key Metrics

During the early stages of program development, it's necessary to develop a set of key metrics that specifically measure the performance of the program implementation, as well as the success in meeting larger organizational goals. Gathering data is usually not difficult. Most organizations have many resources in place to capture extensive amounts of employee data through the use of surveys, proximity card access records, network utilization, policy compliance, employee retention and performance, or real estate costs. The challenge is to first determine the organization's goals for adopting a new, or scaling a legacy, program. The next is to identify the behaviors, transactions, movements, and other factors that best measure program success in achieving those goals.

Organizations successful in implementing Workshift tend to identify metrics that enable them to evaluate the success of the program on two levels: at a program level (e.g., can the organization effectively support employees as they change their way of working?), and at an enterprise level (e.g., do the outcomes of enabling employees to Workshift aid the organization in meeting enterprise-wide goals?).

A good example of leveraging data to measure success toward achieving enterprise goals comes from NovAtel, the world's leading supplier of global navigation satellite system receivers. When the company began looking beyond Canada's borders to expand its development group, there were a myriad of new factors to consider. However, from the beginning, the executives of NovAtel realized that as the organization began to grow internationally Workshift was a strategic initiative for the whole company, not just applicable for a single business unit, and program data needed to support the measurement of progress to enterprise-wide goals.

"It was a big step for the company. It also began the conversation about the changing workplace and showed that we need to pay attention to these changes," explained Tannis Schwarz, director of HR at NovAtel Inc.

Organization Quick Stats

Name: NovAtel
Industry: High tech manufacturing
Year founded: 1978
Description: NovAtel is the world's leading supplier of global navigation satellite system receivers. The company provides precise positioning GPS applications such as surveying, geographic information systems, aviation, marine, mining and machine control, and precision agriculture. NovAtel is continually expanding its global sales and participant service presence, and in 2011, opened a product development site in India, the first development group outside of its headquarters.
Headquarters: Calgary, Alberta, Canada
Region: Global
Number of employees: Approximately 350
Revenue: $50,000,000 ($CDN), 2012
Website: www.novatel.com

The executive team recognized that employees would need to work across different time zones and "traditional" work schedules wouldn't always fit with the demands of a global customer base and the need to support global and distributed teams.

"They understood that innovation doesn't always happen between 8 a.m. and 4:30 p.m. and within the walls of people's offices and cubicles," added Schwarz. "They understood that time is a critical resource and to make the most of everyone's time, NovAtel and its employees need to become flexible."

For NovAtel, implementing Workshift became an executive-level goal that had enterprise-wide impacts. When NovAtel completed their pilot, Schwartz said the results were measurable. Through an employee survey, more than 80 percent reported that they were better able to manage demands of both work and personal commitments, resulting in greater employee satisfaction. Additionally, employees saved 1.67 hours of commute time per week on average. All of this data enabled executives to measure program efficacy as well as track progress on their overall organizational goals. Their organizational goals were then used to identify data points that could be captured during the pilot in order to effectively measure their progress.

"Our goal was to improve productivity, employee engagement and retention, and our ability to attract the talent we need in a highly competitive labor market by providing flexibility in the scheduling and location of work," Schwartz said. "If we could allow people to work when they work best, why not?"

Organizational leaders recognize the importance of well-selected success metrics for their core business and support areas. However, many entities initially struggle to identify appropriate metrics to measure the program's ability to meet enterprise goals and deliver value to the organization. Ideally, program effectiveness should be linked to the overall performance metrics that measure other business and support area results, such as HR, IT, corporate real estate, and enterprise-wide environmental sustainability goals. Organizations with successful programs tend to have the clearest lines of sight from their program data to those overall performance metrics and executive scorecards. This correlates the program to the mix of financial, operational, customer, and learning/growth measures that form leading and lagging indicators of the overall health of the organization.

In the early stages of development, we have found that many organizations measure a variety of areas to gain feedback about the program. For example, the organization may want more immediate feedback to understand if the program is changing organizational culture or meeting resistance. Or, leaders may want to collect information during the pilot phase to further build the business case before expanding the program to a broader audience. However, most program metrics used by successful program managers fall into the following six categories: sustainability/eligibility, participation demographics, training, satisfaction, productivity/performance, and cost savings.

Suitability/Eligibility

In some cases, only a select group of employees in an organization will be suited to participate in a Workshift program and, as a result, are eligible to enter the program. Whether that group is large or small, it's important to understand which employees and job roles are best suited (as well as those who are absolutely not) in order to accurately craft eligible guidelines for program participants. Once guidelines have been established and approved (the HR team typically likes to have input and approval of guidelines affecting employees and the workplace), factors and values are created to enable managers to determine which employees can participate in the program.

Suitability Assessment

In many organizations, telework or flexible work arrangements may not be available for all employees. Some employees may be precluded from enrolling in the program because of job functions

Table 7.1 Eligibility metrics

Type of Metric	*Description*	*How this is used*
Work Role	What category best fits the requirements and interaction level of the employee? For example, does the employee typically work head's down, in a collaborative mode or at a distance from other team members?	The program manager can identify a list of work roles and then make assumptions about each role's eligibility to participate. Role selection should not be a single determining factor, but just one in a series of factors used to suggest eligibility.
Home environment	Does the employee have dedicated space to work at home? Are there constraints in place that would preclude the employee from working effectively from home?	While having dedicated office space should not be a sole requirement for participating, it is a valuable data point in the suitability equation.
Commute distance	What is the employee's current commute distance?	This is important for environmental sustainability reporting, for example, CO_2 emission reduction. In addition to commute distance, some organizations have collected data on type of commute (car, train, ferry, etc), and, for car drivers, the type of vehicle in order to more accurately calculate CO_2 emission avoidance.
Commute cost	An estimate of the current monthly expenses associated with commuting to work.	This is used as an employee cost avoidance metric to market the program internally and to use as a recruiting tool.
Experience	Does the employee have prior experience working from home?	Especially for new hires, it is important to know if the employee has experience, successful or otherwise, in a Workshift arrangement.
Preference	Given the option, does the employee want to Workshift?	It may seem to be a deep insight into the blatantly obvious, but shouldn't we be sure the employee really wants to participate?

or regulatory requirements. Others may be working in roles that are eligible to participate, yet for other reasons they are simply not suited for or do not wish to telework. The challenge is to identify a method to collect enough information to enable a manager to decide whether or not to allow an employee to participate in the program. An assessment can capture information about an employee's role and preferred work style, and this can be shared with the manager to help inform their decision-making process.

The data collected from this process can then be compared with other data on program performance and used to tune the suitability questions to ensure they are accurate predictors of the success of the program participant.

When measuring eligibility, program managers should consider deploying assessment instruments over entire business units or the organization as a whole. By measuring how many employees meet eligibility requirements, program managers can learn valuable information on the overall size of the opportunity and establish more effective and realistic long-term goals for the program (table 7.1).

Participation Demographics

Leaders should understand how many employees are actually enrolled or participating out of the eligible population. If the

Table 7.2 Participation metrics

Type of Metric	*Description*	*How this is used*
Job Title	The employee's standardized job title	Using the organization's established list of job titles enables the program manager to filter data and develop predictive metrics on suitability based on job title.
Organizational Level (if applicable)	Supervisory levels below the organizations most senior executive	This data is critical for approval routing, program impact reporting and business continuity reporting.
Office Location	The primary office shown on employment records	This is an important data point for all utilization impact analysis.
Business Unit/ Department	The name/number of the business unit to which the employee is assigned	This is used to filter data for utilization and program impact reports.
Licenses/Clearances	Any licenses, security clearances or other credentials that could impact an employee's participation in the program	This is used primarily for enrollment approval process and reporting to related outside agencies.

participation to eligibility ratio is low, then leaders will need to identify the underlying factors preventing broader adoption. The ability to drill down to department, process, location, or even the team level can help determine where any potential management resistance is or which employees need more communication or training (table 7.2).

Training

Some organizations have very formal, mandatory training for employees, while other organizations have informal, self-paced, or optional training. Capturing training participation data and assembling transcript reports is valuable in analyzing the correlation between training and performance-related metrics or participation metrics.

Training should be dynamic and nimble, as the program by definition has the ability to adapt rapidly to changing business requirements. Since readiness is a key component of success, it's very important to regularly capture and report feedback from managers and employees on the effectiveness of the training resources. Capturing data on training participation and perceived value becomes vital to ensuring the training program consistently meets evolving requirements.

Satisfaction

Quantitative and qualitative data measuring employee satisfaction, usually obtained through surveys, is very useful to highlight best practices, what's working, and what's not working. Participants and managers may be surveyed separately to understand potential disconnects or teams and departments still struggling with perception issues. Even exit interviews from employees leaving the organization, or just exiting the program, can be used to gather information on what could be done better.

Enrollment Survey

In organizations where Workshift is more formally introduced, the enrollment process is one of the most critical elements in establishing the success of an employee working in given program. Therefore, the final step of their enrollment process is a customer satisfaction survey. The goal of the survey is to determine the efficiency of the enrollment process, the quality and quantity of the information presented and the level of confidence the employee has regarding their ability to be successful in the program.

Employee and Manager Feedback

Many successful programs distribute participant satisfaction surveys to their employees and their managers once or twice each year. In order to derive meaningful information from the survey data, it's important to ask more detailed questions rather than simply asking if participants are satisfied with the program. Specifically, surveys should collect data around satisfaction, accessibility, trending, and open-ended feedback to improve the program (tables 7.3 and 7.4).

Exit Surveys

Exit surveys are a form of satisfaction analysis, and one that is especially critical to program evaluation. Exiting employees may be a valuable source of information to learn how the program can be improved. In some cases, exiting employees may be more open

Table 7.3 Participant survey for managers

Type of Metric	*Description*	*How this is used*
Accessibility	The manager's ability to access employees working remotely	Evaluating program performance
Satisfaction	Overall satisfaction with the program	Evaluating program performance
Satisfaction Trend	Has satisfaction level increased or decreased since last survey	Due to the fluid nature of program participation and survey participation, it can be difficult to effectively measure program satisfaction trends from one survey cycle to the next, or over multiple survey cycles. Adding a survey question to capture the respondents' perception of the direction their satisfaction is trending is a quick way to get a snap shot on program satisfaction progress.
Comments	Open comment field	Some of the most valuable information comes from the data entered by program participants in the comment section. To leverage the best opportunity to gather value from this part of the survey, consider adding prompts such as "tell us the one of the best or one worst aspects of this program." This will help many survey respondents over the writer's block that comes from staring at a blank comment field.

Table 7.4 Participant survey for employees

Type of Metric	*Description*	*How this is used*
Accessibility	The employee's ability to access their manager and team while working remotely	Evaluating program performance
Satisfaction with Program	Overall satisfaction with the program	Evaluating program performance
Satisfaction with Support	Overall satisfaction with the organizations support of their work arrangement.	Typically, this question is broken down into several questions, such as, "What is your satisfaction with the technical support that is provided while you are working remotely?" Additional questions along this line of inquiry may include requests for assessment of touch down space provide when working on site, or teleconferencing capabilities. Adding more questions that pinpoint issues provides better information for the program manager.
Satisfaction Trend	Has satisfaction level increased or decreased since last survey	Due to the fluid nature of program participation and survey participation, it can be difficult to effectively measure program satisfaction trends from one survey cycle to the next, or over multiple survey cycles. Adding a survey question to capture the respondents' perception of the direction their satisfaction is trending is a quick way to get a snap shot on program satisfaction progress.
Comments	Open comment field	Some of the most valuable information comes from the data entered by program participants in the comment section. To leverage the best opportunity to gather value from this part of the survey, consider adding prompts such as "tell us the one of the best or worst aspects of of this program." This will help many survey respondents over the writer's block that comes from staring at a blank comment field.

and direct with their feedback since they have no concerns that the information may be held against them. There is no reason to toe the party line or couch their comments.

The same questions used in the participation survey can be used in the exit survey, with only slight modifications. For example, when including a section for open-ended comments, additional prompts can be added, including, "What aspects of this program would affect your decision to leave or stay with the organization?" To obtain more detailed feedback, we suggest conducting an exit interview in lieu of a survey when feasible. The interviewer can dive more deeply into specific issues that may be of interest or improve the program.

Productivity versus Performance

Frequently we are asked, "How do I measure the productivity of my teleworkers (or participants in a flexible work arrangement)?" It is one of the most important questions, not just for program implementation, but for business performance measurement in general. As Sheldon Dyck, president of ATB Investor Services says, "Productivity is one of the fundamental measures of innovation and the output of an organization. The problem is that too many organizations don't understand yet what are they asking people to do and how to measure their progress. That is a business problem, not just a Workshift problem!"

For Sheldon, effectively measuring productivity is vital.

> "The challenge of measuring productivity has nothing to do with people shifting to a new way of working and everything to do with poor leadership and management. If you can't measure the productivity of the people in your organization you have no chance of becoming excellent whether your labor force is down the hall or in another country. If you don't know whether the people in your company are productive or not how do you know who to reward, who to promote, who to train others to emulate? You have much bigger challenges that you need to solve quickly. You don't know what you're asking people to do so how do they know what to deliver? That is a leadership problem that needs to be solved no matter what type of environment you're going to work in."

This leads us to our common response when asked how to measure the productivity of virtual employees: "How are you measuring your employees right now?" Ideally, there should be no difference. Whether your employees are working two cubicles over from your office or they are across the country working virtually, the goals, objectives, success metrics, or work deliverables should be the same.

Productivity is usually an important callout for managers and can also be obtained through surveys and interviews. Productivity is usually a very subjective metric, indicating how employees feel about their productivity, and is usually tied to their overall job satisfaction.

First, start with the job description. Every employee typically has some sort of job description. If nothing else, there is usually a requisition available on the organization's intranet site that was used to hire the employee. Strip away the jargon and the fluff and it becomes easier to translate it into tangible deliverables. For example, a job description for a business analyst may include something like, "Communicate status and results to the respective stakeholders, including items discussed, actionable items, documenting expectations, and results." Translation: the person takes meeting minutes. Lots of 'em. The employee's manager may expect the team meeting results to be published within 24 hours of every weekly meeting in XYZ format. Whatever the expectation is can become something the manager can measure. This thought process can be used throughout the rest of the job description to help develop clear deliverables.

Next, consider the team or department goals. What are the milestones or interim objectives in reaching the overall goals? Productivity can be correlated to how efficiently those targets are achieved. In certain transactional environments, productivity may be easier to quantify. There may be certain expectations around how much volume an employee can handle over time. For example, a loan processor for a bank may review an average number of loan applications per week or a call center representative may answer an average number of customer inquiries per hour or day. Historical information might be available that can be used as a baseline to compare productivity of in-house employees to virtual workers.

The virtual work environment can make organizations more productive because it forces managers to focus more on results. Many proponents include the reduction of absenteeism as one of the key benefits in the business case for the program. However, the reduction of presenteeism is also a key benefit. Traditionally, presenteeism has referred to the costs associated with employees who work while sick. Today, we use it as a term to describe the impact of employees who are supposed to be working but are completely unproductive. In many large organizations, employees can "work the system" and get by with producing very little work as long as they are physically present in the office building for long hours, creating the perception that they are working. As Sheldon puts it, "You are just kidding yourself that because someone's car is in the parking lot at the right hour or that they are in the office late at night that they are creating value."

It can be a game people can play as long as leadership within the organization does not try to quantify performance. In a Workshift office setting, the value employees bring to the table has to be clear and tangible.

Cost Savings

Cost savings can be measured in a variety of ways from real estate savings to travel cost reduction. This may be the most important metric for senior management and help bolster the business case for greater adoption. All Workshift initiatives need to have some way of quantifying cost savings for leaders of an organization to commit to transforming a culture and moving these initiatives forward.

Over time, implementation metrics may become less and less important as the program becomes ingrained in the culture and is just how business is done. However, initially it is a good idea to select metrics to gauge how well your organization is getting to that desired state.

Different Phases, Different Metrics

A program moves through defined phases as it evolves and matures. While some data points will be important when measuring the efficacy of the program at any point, many tie in with the specific programs goals for completion of a given program implementation phase and successful migration to the next. Consider the following:

Investigate/Discover

One of the primary goals of the Investigate and Discover stages is to gather data necessary to craft a business case that supports the implementation of a formal program. In addition, this baseline data will be used to validate program success and to identify opportunities and challenges associated with scaling the program.

A Workshift program touches all areas within an organization, and it impacts data in many of the organization's different business and support areas. Capturing data to create the business case requires the program designer to identify which business unit data, such as HR, corporate real estate, and IT, is currently used to quantify space and resource utilization as well as overall performance.

While it would seem that there would be an industry-wide approach to measuring resource use, the goals of the business typically drive which metrics are most important to use in demonstrating positive impacts. For example, many financial services companies are highly motivated to drive reductions in real estate and occupancy expenses. Conversely, we have found that some companies in the energy generation sector are motivated to provide a workplace that attracts talent in a highly competitive employment market.

While the weighting of the factors varies among industries, from both private- and public-sector perspectives, we believe there are several key factors to gather data during the Investigate and Discover phases (tables 7.5 and 7.6).

When is a square foot not a square foot?

Space measurement in corporate real estate is used to assess the value of a property and to distribute the cost of occupancy equitably to each occupant of a building.

While there are several different approaches to measuring space within a commercial building or property, the most commonly used methodology was developed and is maintained by the Building Owners and Manager's Association International or BOMA.

For more detailed information on commercial building measurement, we recommend that you go to BOMA's website at www.boma.org.

Design/Engage

The primary focus of data collection during the Design and Engage stages is to capture enough information to accurately test an organization's ability to effectively support employee, manager,

Table 7.5 Real estate metrics

Type of Metric	*Description*	*Equation*	*Comments*	*Notes*
Current Annual Rentable[1] Square Foot (RSF) Rate for Each Location[2]	Annual cost per RSF	Total Annual Rent & Occupancy[3] (R&O) Cost/RSF by Location	Building the business case for a formal program begins with gathering baseline data on existing corporate real estate costs. Subsequent assumptions of cost savings related to reducing the real estate footprint can be factored against these baseline costs to identify "hard dollar" savings.	1. Rentable square footage is the area of space that a landlord uses to determine rent fees. 2. If the organization occupies multiple locations, it is important to gather this data for all locations. The goal is to build an "apples to apples" comparison of occupancy costs across the enterprise, such that strategic decisions can be made later in the process regarding pilot, launch and scale decisions. 3. Occupancy costs typically include utilities, repairs, common area maintenance (CAM), capital project amortization and security expenses to name a few. Be sure to understand what expenses are baked into the rent and occupancy (R&O) value you use for your analysis.
OPTIONAL: Projected Annual RSF Rate for Each Location[4]	Projected annual cost per RSF	Total R&O Cost/ RSF by Location by Future Year[5]	R&O costs change over time. In most cases, R&O will increase year to year, but a burn off of capital amortization[6] or an increase in cost savings measures associated with other corporate real estate initiatives are examples o f ways in which R&O can reduce over time. If the corporate real estate team can provide projections of annual R&O costs, it will lead to a more accurate forecast of a program's positive impact on corporate expenses over time.	4. If the organization occupies multiple locations, it is important to gather this data for all locations. The goal is to build an "apples to apples" comparison of occupancy costs across the enterprise, such that strategic decisions can be made later in the process regarding pilot, launch and scale decisions. 5. Annual projections of expenses should follow the organization's standard for financial reporting, specifically using either fiscal or calendar year when appropriate. 6. Capital amortization is the allocation of a capital project's expenses to annual periods over a given period of time. When a project has been fully amortized, the associated expense is no longer paid.

Current RSF per Occupant[7]	Amount of space required to support each employee assigned to a given work location	Location RSF[8]/# of Occupants	Another key factor of the baseline analysis is data that quantifies current utilization of real estate resources. One of the natural outcomes of a successful program is an increase in the number of location occupants. In fact, occupants assigned to a location can exceed the number of seats[9] available.	7. "Occupant" is defined as an employee who is assigned to a given location. Typically, all employees (even mobile road warriors or legacy teleworkers) are assigned to a company location. This is usually done for tax purposes. Human Resources is the most likely source of this information. 8. The RSF per Occupant value should only use the RSF for the Occupants occupied location, not the portfolio wide RSF. 9. "Seats" is a term used to identify the total number of employees that can work concurrently and still occupy a unique workstation or office.
Current Annual R&O Cost per Occupant	The R&O cost required to support each employee assigned to a given work location	Total R&O Costs of a Location/ Total Occupants of the Same Location[10]	This metric provides more information on the true cost of each location and further helps to target the work locations that would be the first priority during Pilot, Launch and Scale program phases.	10. This factor should only include the R&O costs and occupants of a specific location and not of the overall enterprise wide R&O, unless the enterprise wide R&O costs are distributed proportionately across the portfolio
Current Annual R&O Cost per Office per Location[11]	The average R&O cost of an office in each location.	Average Office RSF[12] Building R&O rate per RSF	This metric highlights the disparity in the cost of occupancy between workstations and private offices. This metric helps with the cost justification of reconfiguring private offices as touch down spaces for mobile employees as it shows an increased utilization of space that is typically more expensive than workstations and other touch down space.	11. While there may be some value to understanding the enterprise wide cost of an office or workstation, organizations with large real estate footprints typically have a range of R&O expenses that is too broad to interpret a metric of "average" effectively. 12. Average Office RSF is determined by listing the RSF of every office at a given location and calculating the average value. If the location has a small number of unusually sized offices, the RSF for those spaces may be excluded although any charts using this data should footnote the omission.
R&O cost per workstation	The average R&O cost of workstation in each location.	Average Workstation RSF[13] Building R&O rate per RSF		13. Workstation is defined as any unique workspace that is assigned to an employee, or in the instance of a call center or similar shared workspace environment, to a group of employees. Private offices are not considered in the workstation value.

Table 7.6 Human capital costs

Type of Metric	*Description*	*Equation*	*Comments*	*Notes*
Talent acquisition cost	The average cost to add a new employee to the organization	The inputs for this metric will vary from organization to organization. Online tools (i.e. ADP) tools are available and provide a free calculators[14] to determine an estimated cost of talent acquisition.	Employee retention is one of the key benefits identified when proposing the implementation of a Workshift program. Therefore, it is important to quantify the cost associated with talent acquisition and, thereby, the cost avoidance associated with the benefit of retaining employees.	14. The online calculator can be found on the ADP webpage (www.adp.com)
Total voluntary turnover rate/attrition	The annual rate at which employees voluntarily terminate their employment with the organization.	# of Employees Voluntarily Resigning Annually/Total Employee Headcount[15]	This metric provides a different view to support that Workshift positively impacts employee retention. The cost of attrition, while being a hard dollar expense, involves a calculation with many variables (lost cost of recruiting and training, as well as the cost to repopulate the vacant position). Because these variables typically differ for each organization, it is difficult to accurately compare attrition costs between organizations. Therefore, while the cost of attrition may not be associated with a comparable value of hard dollar savings, it does provide a quantitative value for the program efficacy.	15. Typically this metric is used to reference an enterprise wide impact. For greater clarity, the value can be further distilled to a location by location analysis.
OPTIONAL: Organizational Culture Results		The values for this metric come directly from the results of the organizational culture assessment.	For organizations that formally assess employee perception of workplace culture, the data can be used to assess baseline information for later studies on program efficacy. One cautionary note: Organizational culture surveys tend to draw conclusions by assessing a broad range of factors. As such, it may be difficult to attribute changes in the assessment scores year over year to the impact of the program alone.	

and organizational needs. Typically, a primary source of data for measurement during these phases is a pilot.

By definition, a pilot is an activity that involves a small sample of the overall organizational population, and uses data collected from the sample to test assumptions or hypothesis. For example, one company we spoke with established three hypothesis during their pilot:

1. 75 percent of pilot participants would remain in the program through the duration of the pilot.
2. 65 percent of pilot participants would rate their satisfaction with the program as 4 or higher on a 5-point Likert scale, with "4" being "satisfied" and "5" being "highly satisfied."
3. 150 employees would enroll in the pilot.

Data used during the pilot was used to accept each of the pilot's hypotheses, quantitatively label the pilot as being successful, and propel the program to the next phase.

While this approach is somewhat simple, we believe additional factors should be used to determine the organization's readiness to migrate from the Design and Engage phases to Launch (table 7.7).

Launch/Scale

While an organization may experience a successful pilot, launching the program to a larger population can create many unanticipated consequences. Although it is impossible to anticipate all of the issues and outcomes of launching enterprise-wide, successful programs have numerous litmus tests to continuously and effectively measure their health and growth.

The challenge in capturing data during the Launch and Scale stages is to balance a program team's seemingly inexhaustible need for information with program participants' need to be left alone to do their work. Participation can be grouped into four distinct phases:

- Suitability
- Enrollment/on-boarding
- Management
- Exit

Table 7.7 Satisfaction metrics

Type of Metric	*Description*	*Equation*	*Comments*	*Notes*
Employee Satisfaction	Employee satisfaction with the pilot, including on-boarding, management approval, provisioning and training	Data captured in an Employee Pre- and Post Enrollment Satisfaction Survey[16]	There are many facets to the program and distilling the assessment of satisfaction to picking a number between 1 and 5 does not provide all the information necessary to successfully capture lessons learned from the pilot.	16. Capturing data during the pilot phases is critical for the success of the Launch and Scale phases. Therefore, pilot participants should be required to complete the assessment as a condition of their participation.
Manager Satisfaction	Manager satisfaction with the pilot, including manger specific communications, team impact and interaction with the participating employee	Data captured in a Manager Pre- and Post Enrollment Satisfaction Survey[17]	Although they may remain in the office in a traditional work environment during the pilot, managers of employees are as much a part of the program as their employees. In fact, data collected from the managers will provide additional depth to the analysis of the pilot's success.	17. Managers will often have more than one employee enrolled in the program. To avoid the negative effective of receiving multiple versions of the same survey, consider having manager's submit a single survey to evaluate their overall experience with the program.
Exit Interview – Employee and Manager	Quantitative and qualitative measure of the employee and manager's opinion of the program and reason for withdrawal	Data captured in Employee and Manager Program Exit Survey	In addition to learning information that might be used to improve the pilot, and eventually the full implementation, the Exit Survey prevents assumptions regarding the cause of attrition. One organization found that people left the pilot for reasons unrelated to program participation (e.g. one was promoted to a new role that was not compatible with participating in the pilot). While it was never confirmed, the employee believed her promotion was directly related to her improved performance, which she believed was enabled by participating in the program.	

The program team can then assign discreet data collection exercises to each program phase (table 7.8).

Table 7.8 Suitability

Type of Metric	*Description*	*Equation*	*Comments*
Suitability Assessment	Employees complete an on-line survey that measures their suitability to participate in the program.	The assessment captures data on over 40 different factors, including preferred work style, current role responsibilities and preferred work arrangement.	Upon completion of the assessment, the employee views the results and decides whether or not to pursue their interest to participate in the program. If they do so, they forward the results to their manager. The manager can view the results, as well as information to assist them in interpreting the assessment scores. This allows both the employee and the manager to make an informed decision on the employee's suitability for the program.

In addition to providing valuable information necessary to make effective, data-driven decisions on program participation, the suitability assessment data can be leveraged to boost workplace utilization by enabling the corporate real estate team to make more strategic leasing and design decisions (tables 7.9–7.11).

Table 7.9 Enrollment/on-boarding

Type of Metric	*Description*	*Equation*	*Comments*
On-Boarding Pre- and Post Survey	At two points in the enrollment and on-boarding process, employees are asked to complete a survey to assess their current understanding of the program and their satisfaction with the enrollment and on-boarding process.	The assessment captures data on close to 10 different factors, including current opinions and proposed process improvements. In addition, the survey attempts to assess conventional wisdom about the program so that program information websites and communications can be improved to provide better information to potential participants.	The data capture here supports continuous process improvement and enables the team to monitor the process for efficacy and rapidly adapt enrollment and on-boarding to changing employee and business requirements.

Table 7.10 Management

Type of Metric	*Description*	*Equation*	*Comments*	*Notes*
Bi-Annual Employee and Manager Participant Satisfaction Survey	Twice each year, employees and managers[18] are invited to participate in a 10 to 15 question survey designed to assess their satisfaction with their participation in the program.	The on-line survey uses a standard set of questions every time it is deployed to enable the team to track changes to data over time. However, the survey will also include a few questions to assess point-in-time issues that may impact one or two survey cycles.	The results of this instrument have been the single most effective tool in successfully making in-flight adjustments to the programs resources and processes, as well as promoting the efficacy of the program internally and externally.	18. Managers will often have more than one employee enrolled in the program. To avoid the negative effective of receiving multiple versions of the same survey, consider having manager's submit a single survey to evaluate their overall experience with the program.
Manager's Quarterly Review	Four times per year, managers are prompted to complete an on-line assessment of their opinion of the continued efficacy of the employee's work arrangement[19].	The assessment captures data on five factors to enable the manager to judge the effectiveness of the work arrangement over time.	The key component of this assessment is the fact that work arrangement is being measured, not employee performance. Therefore, the goal is not to measure employee productivity, but whether the work arrangement is still effective in meeting both the employee and manager's goals.	19. Unlike other surveys that require manager participation, managers receive one survey for each employee.

Table 7.11 Exit

Type of Metric	*Description*	*Equation*	*Comments*
Exit Interview – Employee and Manager	Quantitative and qualitative measure of the employee and manager's opinion of the program and reason for withdrawal	Data captured in Employee and Manager Program Exit Survey	In addition to learning information that might be used to improve the program, the Exit Survey prevents assumptions regarding the cause of attrition.

One Size Does Not Fit All

The primary program stakeholder is different in every organization. Whether the driving force behind the program is corporate real estate, HR, or IT, or a combination thereof, the success measures and achievement milestones will differ from program to program based on the program owner's position in the organization. For example, one organization may measure success based upon the ratio of real estate square footage to head count. Another organization may look at recruitment, retention, or performance evaluations as a program success indicator. At a macro level, overall corporate performance metrics may also impact success measurements. Additionally, organizations with growth goals will have far different benchmarks than those retracting in size and focused on cost reduction.

In this chapter, we have covered a variety of metrics that specifically address the progress of the initiative. Keep in mind, goals may change over time and corresponding metrics of success may then change too. Organizations should be flexible enough to accommodate the change in metrics or at least the change in the targets for established metrics. As the organization evolves, success metrics may give way to broader organizational measures that evaluate the overall health of the business. This is a natural maturation as Workshift will not be considered as a separate, stand-alone initiative, but will ultimately become a natural component of how business is conducted within the organization.

Stage 6: Measure—Summary

Key activities in this phase are:

- Measuring success metrics
- Recurring reports to senior management and the rest of the organization
- Highlighting and communicating success stories and best practices

Deliverables:

- Documented success stories
- Documented success metrics

Key risks:

- Lack of management involvement in reviewing metrics
- Inability to capture data
- Success stories are not communicated
- The tools for enterprise-wide sharing are not made available

CHAPTER 8

Leverage

If you are deliberately trying to create a future that feels safe, you will willfully ignore the future that is likely.

—Seth Godin

Up to this point, we focused on describing the process of designing, implementing, and scaling a successful program. We discussed the benefits and illustrated the positive impacts by describing processes and sharing stories of the challenges overcome and successes realized by a number of organizations. We reviewed reported results that indicated tangible benefits: improved scores on organizational employee culture studies, decreases in attrition, or cost savings related to reductions in real estate or talent acquisition costs. Across the board, we heard from program leaders that employees and teams who participated in some way functioned better or were generally improved after formally adopting a program. While we were not surprised to hear leaders report these results, we were curious to learn exactly how much better the *organizations* were after formal adoption, and if some improved significantly more or realized greater benefits than others. Specifically, were some organizations experiencing the commonly advertised benefits while others found something more... perhaps even much more?

We were also curious as to whether there was a distinction between programs that were scaling in size and growing, and those that were discovering new, perhaps unanticipated benefits to their business based on their ability to successfully enable their employees to work anywhere. We call this "leveraging Workshift." By looking closer at the beneficial results reported by most organizations, we found most fell into the "successfully made the workplace better for employees" category, and some resulted in a degree of improvement realized by the organization. However, a few organizations, including those that we discuss in this chapter, realized significant and quantifiable benefits by leveraging results. And, when they did, it delivered significant dividends on the organization's investment.

In order to understand how organizations that successfully leveraged results were different than others, we began by first studying how they were the same.

In the Beginning...

The catalyst for implementation within the organizations we studied typically began more with "acceptance management" rather than "change management." Change management, popular in many companies, is the process of changing attitudes, behaviors, and practices of employees and teams within organizations. The required change is typically directed from senior levels, and a comprehensive plan is developed that includes selling an idea to all levels within the organization. Acceptance management is a bit more subtle. Behaviors or work practices may already be changing within the organization, and leadership is then tasked with understanding how to build on the momentum. Unlike most new workplace programs in an organization, it tends not to begin with someone saying, "Let's do something different," but more often began with an idea to "do something we are already doing... but do it better."

Typically a formal approach to flex work started or gained momentum when a business leader working in some department within the organization realized employees were working outside of the office, or realized the extent to which employees were working off-site. It may have been a few employees here and there, or it may have been an entire team. At that time the leader hypothesized that the organization was likely not realizing significant benefits from those work arrangements, other than benefiting the employees and their managers at some level, or else those work arrangements would never be established. But, was the organization really quantifiably better because of it? And if so, how? For the organizations we studied, the asking and answering of these questions were the genesis of their more formalized program, and this was the same for those organizations that were and were not really leveraging their program's benefits.

From there, program adoption continued along the path we describe in this book's previous chapters. The organizations studied, created, tested, implemented, and, for the most part, realized the benefits they anticipated at their program's inception. Employees responded with higher scores on culture surveys, managers reported higher levels of productivity without a corresponding loss of connectivity and collaboration, and the organization had the ability to attract talent in labor markets previously inaccessible while retaining talent that may have left to find increased work flexibility elsewhere. However, it is at this point where the differentiation between organizations that realized benefits and those that leveraged them, takes place. The consistent point of departure with each of these organizations is the emergence of a "*burning platform.*"

When More Is More

In mid-2008, the financial crisis in the United States was in full swing. Financial services firms and companies in other business sectors were off-boarding employees at a vigorous pace. Other organizations were merging or disappearing altogether, and executives were scrambling to find ways to cut expenses.

As the financial crisis gained momentum late in 2008, the corporate real estate (CRE) team for one large financial services company looked for ways to deliver cost savings. The CRE team examined their current rent and occupancy costs, and studied ways to reduce them. One of the largest corporate spaces also happened to be one of the most expensive, located in New York City. The cost of the space made it an attractive focus for discussions on ways to maximize the utilization of the work environment while reducing the overall quantity of space. The puzzle facing the CRE team was whether they could use less of this very expensive real estate without losing key employees or negatively impacting corporate culture. They thought: Could the space be reduced, but not the people? And if so, could the number of people participating in the company's telework program be expanded?

Earlier that same year, the firm launched their telework program with the goal of better supporting employees consistently working remotely and reducing real estate costs by optimizing the space previously assigned to employees now working primarily from home. While the program management team, a cross-functional team comprised of director level managers from business units, including HR, CRE, information security, IT, and risk management, identified cost savings opportunities in their business case seeking approval to launch the program, no one anticipated the extent of savings the program would contribute when the time came to really leverage it.

In May 2008, just a few months prior to the time when the financial crisis really began to ripple through the financial markets, the company successfully piloted and began a small scope implementation of their program. A key component of the program was that all participating employees were required to give up their assigned workspace completely, or to move into a single workspace assigned to multiple employees. In the first month of the pilot project, 24 seats were permanently vacated, freeing up the equivalent of $244,000 in rent and occupancy costs. This savings was a top measure of program success.

The CRE team reviewed the results of the pilot and reasoned that if the program could create such significant vacant space during the pilot alone, then launching the program to a larger population could create an immediate and significant inventory of available space on a broader scale. If the CRE and program team could partner together to focus on the New York office, IT, HR, and corporate services support resources could be delivered more efficiently than simply implementing in numerous locations across the country. The result would be the CRE team leveraging vacancies, along with vacancies created by implementing other workplace programs (smaller workstations, reducing circulation inefficiency), to create large sections of sub-leasable space in New York.

The CRE team quickly calculated that the sublease rates, even in a market heavily impacted by the growing economic downturn, would more than cover the related expenses and deliver significant annual cost savings for the firm.

As the teams worked together with leadership from all of the firm's business units to develop a revised occupancy plan for the

New York office, the Workshift team in the New York office began the task of actively promoting the value and benefit of participating in the program. Based on their anecdotal evidence that many New York-based employees were already working from home at least part-time, the CRE and program teams determined that focusing on formalizing existing telework arrangements, and enrolling those employees eager to work remotely, would significantly contribute to the number of vacancies required to support the CRE team's business case for cost savings.

As vacancies were created by enrollment in the program and through the results of other workplace programs, the CRE team "restacked" the building, relocating employees and teams to create or improve the functional and organizational adjacencies that tend to be lost as organizations contract or grow. This process helped to better align remaining teams and consolidate vacancies into leasable tracts of space. In addition, the company implemented several projects to convert their single-tenant facility into a multi-tenant building. Although the work to restack and reconfigure the building was a significant expense, the newly available space was leased to several tenants within six months, netting the firm almost $19 million in rent and occupancy savings each year.

The opportunity to save $19 million was not a part of the original program charter, nor was this dramatic cost savings generated exclusively by the program. However, the firm would not have realized the net benefits had flexible work not been implemented earlier and, more importantly, if program results had not been aligned with other workplace strategies to generate significant cost savings. As this case shows, organizations that implement Workshift programs, even small programs, are helping to future-proof their organization.

Scaling with Speed

Using a burning platform (in this case, a global financial crisis) as the catalyst to rapidly scale an existing program is the common thread in organizations that successfully leverage the value of Workshift. Approaches used to create that leverage are often very different, yet interestingly yield similar results.

The aforementioned financial services company – responded to their need to quickly generate significant cost savings by scaling their existing telework program by leveraging more of an "acceptance management" approach. Many of the program participants had only worked remotely on occasion and some had an interest in doing so prior to enrolling in the program. But, what if the company already had a significant number of employees working from home and still had assigned space they were not using? Could they have leveraged their program more quickly and realized savings faster?

WellPoint had a similar compelling opportunity to reduce their CRE footprint. However, at the time their burning platform opportunity surfaced, WellPoint already had an established Workshift program in place, with high participation rates. The WellPoint team used a different approach to migrating employees from assigned offices and work stations to working exclusively from home. Affected employees were already working outside the office and did not need to transition to a new way of working; however, to realize the bottom-line benefits of the program, the organization needed employees to make a complete transition that included forfeiting their underutilized desks. Therefore, WellPoint decided not to deploy an extensive change management program. WellPoint's Workshift program, officially known as Off Premise Workers, or OPW, encouraged employees to work remotely rather than occupying workspace on-site. During 2011, WellPoint's CRE team began the process of evaluating their strategy to address a rapidly approaching deadline for the renewal of the lease in one of the organization's large campuses. The CRE team kicked off the process with a three-month due diligence exercise to determine the feasibility of renewing all or a portion of their lease for the property. After conducting qualitative observation analysis and quantitative research using key card access and other data, the CRE team determined that almost 1,500 employees were using their assigned workstations less than 40 percent of the time, or approximately four days every two weeks.

Armed with this information, WellPoint's CRE team calculated revised space requirements, adding the new assumption that employees working from home more than working on-site would release their assigned workspaces. The result of this analysis was the realization that the organization could cut the amount of space they occupied on that campus by 60 percent and still meet workplace resource needs for the population supported by the campus.

The annual cost savings to lease 60 percent less space would equate to more than $40 million!

Once the CRE team calculated the financial impact of leasing less space, they realized they needed executive support to implement a plan for OPW employees to move out, and have their space reconfigured to more efficiently accommodate a smaller on-site worker population. With 45 days to design and execute this plan before their lease expired, the team needed to move fast.

Not surprisingly, once the executive team learned the net cost savings (reduced rent and occupancy costs less project expenses) and reviewed how the space was actually used, the decision to support the project to rapidly move OPW employees out of underutilized space on-site came quickly.

The CRE team began the sprint to move 1,500 people working in the OPW program out of their assigned desks on-site. WellPoint, unlike many other organizations we spoke with, followed a very direct approach to scaling their program to realize significant value for the organization, specifically:

1. Managers and employees were notified by email that the campus was being consolidated and those not working on-site full time were being moved into the OPW program.
2. Although the WellPoint HR team was consulted on the process, they were not the process owners. Since people were already teleworking, WellPoint was eliminating access to a resource, a workplace resource, which was not being fully utilized. Therefore it was deemed primarily a real estate issue, not a HR issue.

Discerning what type of space to provide employees when they were required to or desired to come back to the office for meetings became a larger question. WellPoint's architectural vendor designed touchdown space for use by workshifting employees when working on-site, but surprisingly, the WellPoint CRE team learned that even that space was underutilized by the population for which it was intended. After studying utilization of space, the WellPoint CRE team learned temporary contractors mostly used the space, and visiting employees typically found space in conference rooms and other spaces within their departmental areas. This caused the

CRE team to reconsider what designated touchdown space should look like for their corporate culture.

Research has been conducted and continues to examine the temporal flow of people, work process, and information between different work modes and activity behaviors. The quality of workspace integration is the degree to which the workspace facilitates the seamless flow of people and information across work modes.[1] WellPoint was only able to discern what space configuration worked best for its employees by studying the utilization of space. By doing so, WellPoint was successful in leveraging their program to realize significant benefits and value that were not anticipated at the program's inception.

A Global Company Spawns Collaborative Tools

BroadVision, a Redwood City, California-based company is a leader in cloud-based solutions for the virtual workplace. In developing their main collaborative tool, Clearvale, Lisa Lyssand, VP of HR and facilities shared that, "Before using this tool, we didn't have an easy way of communicating with remote employees. We had a hard time navigating a portal product that made it difficult to process forms of communication. We had limited employees having access and a lot of meetings being held for managers to be connected to remote workers that took a lot of time for them. This gave managers a long working day because they were touching base with employees and clients in Europe in the morning, in the Americas during the day, and in Asia during in the evening. Executives were struggling with these limitations."

Organization Quick Stats

Name: BroadVision
Industry: Internet services: Online commerce and business social networking solutions
Year founded: 1993
Description: BroadVision has been a global leader in providing organizations with the rules, tools, and infrastructure for doing business on the web. BroadVision Clearvale, is a leader in cloud-based solutions for the virtual, mobile, social enterprise.

Headquarters: Redwood City, California
Region: Global
Number of employees: Approximately 200
Revenue: $52.3 million, 2012
Website: www.broadvision.com

While BroadVision has a flexible work policy along with guidelines on how to request it, the way it's managed is informal. Employees initiate conversations with managers, and most of the departments have flexible work schedules. For California-based employees, it is routine to spend at least one day a week from home or work flexible hours by working from home in the mornings and coming into the office in the afternoon, largely because it's accepted in the culture, and largely from the desire to circumvent traffic congestion in a major urban area.

"Clearvale evolved from a previous product, an interactive HR portal page, and has been in use for five years now. The tool links everyone together so well," Lisa said. "My managers can see what everybody is doing no matter where they are, and employees can post documents that everyone in the international workforce can work on in their time zone. Managers can go in the next day to view changes, comments, and the flow of information from BroadVision's CEO, Pehong Chen, to all employees."

The ability to open up communications this way has moved BroadVision away from silos as a company. Using this tool was "a turning point in our corporate history as it wasn't just our CEO telling his executives his vision. He now promotes a bi-directional communication process and gets firsthand communication from everyone in the workforce," Lisa added. BroadVision does not officially have an office for international employees because they are working in a mobile way or from home offices. The CEO models this flexibility as he works from home every morning then comes into the office later in the afternoon, and heads home to work with Beijing, China, in the evening.

In assessing space utilization, BroadVision recently moved their headquarters to a smaller, more efficient office. The company realized they did not need cubicles for everybody and sought to offer more meeting rooms and hotel room stations.

"Of the cubicles we did have," Lisa shared, "we made them low in the middle, and put in hotel areas around them so employees could sit somewhere to plug in if needed. Now we have extra meeting room space for team or client meetings, a definite change from what we had before. We received a lot of positive feedback among staff that this newly designed space fostered a natural collaboration."

For BroadVision, developing and deploying a collaborative tool successfully helped the organization turn a corner in supporting a more mobile workforce. It was through realizing the benefits of this tool that the company achieved far more efficiencies than ever envisioned before.

This outcome is supported by recent findings from a recent McKinsey Global Survey that identified characteristics of a networked enterprise and the outsized benefits many companies are realizing from leveraging social, collaborative tools. Nine out of ten executives surveyed, whose organizations use social tools, reported some measurable business benefit with employees, customers, and business partners. From a financial perspective, respondents reported that social tools contribute 20 percent and 18 percent, respectively, to all the revenue increases and cost improvements their companies attribute to the use of all digital technologies.[2]

The use of social technologies has, in anticipated and unanticipated ways, dramatically changed how companies organize and manage themselves, giving rise to the need for more redesigned business processes and a fundamental shift in how the nature of work is done.

An Entrepreneur Tackles Remote Work—In a Big Way!

Jim Ball is the former founder and CEO of Alpine Access, a Denver, Colorado-based provider of distributed workforce call center solutions that was acquired by a larger service provider in 2012. During his career, Jim gained extensive experience leading traditional contact center environments, and over time, he observed that the call handling industry was experiencing two significant challenges:

1. Extensive turnover rates of call center employees, and
2. The pervasive negative impacts on call center business operations from clients threatening to offshore call handling functions.

Jim understood that the inherent nature of the contact center business was that client needs were volatile, swinging wildly from high to low demand for call handling services. At the same time, he was keenly aware of the challenges of meeting the fluid nature of his clients' business requirements with the small supply of skilled workers who were available at attractive wage rates in the areas where most call center facilities were located.

Over time, Jim wondered if there was a way to tap into the population of skilled workers who lived in areas beyond existing service center locations in order to efficiently expand his team and the flexibility of his service delivery. He knew that smaller communities were competing with one another by providing aggressive financial incentives to attract contact center businesses to boost employment. He also realized there was a problem in that the pool of suitable talent within a reasonable radius of one of these individual communities alone was often too small to meet a client's business requirements. This meant that the current model to staff and support smaller contact centers often did not match reality of the clients' needs. But what if there was a way to aggregate the resources in each of these smaller communities into a larger team, without the need to place people shoulder to shoulder in the same building?

Ball continued to study the situation over the years and eventually reengineered the established approach of providing call center services by using workers staffing existing hub locations, and created a model where a client's calls were serviced with a dedicated team of workers distributed in numerous locations.

Organization Quick Stats

Name: Alpine Access
Industry: Customer service
Year founded: 1998 (acquired in 2012)
Description: Alpine Access offered a robust suite of distributed workforce solutions and capabilities, including virtual contact center services, Software-as-a-Solution (SaaS) based talent management platforms and services, security solutions in the cloud, and consulting services.

Headquarters: Denver, Colorado, United States of America
Region: North America
Number of employees: Over 3,000

The result of Jim's work was Alpine Access, an organization designed to not only realize the benefits of a virtual work environment, but also leverage it as their company's differentiator in an industry that traditionally required employees to work on-site. Jim built his organization by implementing a new staffing strategy that embraced the following premise: In order to be successful building a team comprised exclusively of remote call handlers, constructing an infrastructure of resources that supported a work environment in which there was no reason to come on-site would be required. Ball believed the model without this would inevitably break because, once again, the business would become restricted to geography.

Jim and his leadership team realized they would need to recruit the highest qualified customer service representatives to support this new business model. Ball also recognized that the added value of a distributed team would come with an added responsibility for his organization: better management. (It's interesting to note that other leaders in organizations we spoke with also cited better management as an additional benefit. To manage virtual employees, managers had to become better at setting expectations, communicating clearly, and measuring results rather than attendance.)

The Alpine Access team quickly learned that opening hiring to more geographic areas by enabling remote work made the acquisition of a more qualified team much easier. It even yielded an unanticipated benefit that made measuring the efficacy of this new approach much easier: Customers identified the benefits for them!

By opening their search for new employees to almost every geographic area, Alpine Access was able to find call center representatives who were genuinely interested in the products and services their clients provided. Jim reported that some clients saw as much as a 30 percent increase in sales, believed to be attributed to the higher quality of the Alpine Access team.

For Alpine Access, the organization benefits are tangible and significant, but it required formal commitment and investment from the organization. In Ball's opinion, many traditional, brick-and-mortar business leaders do not clearly understand all their current internal issues so it's no surprise they are reluctant about an unknown work arrangement such as remote work.

"If you're interested in implementing a distributed work model, you need to do some serious blocking and tackling on the issues your business faces today," Ball said. "Applying the change management and business process improvements required to successfully implement, and truly leverage the value of a telework program, will significantly improve your business, even if your employees are not working remotely."

Governments and Workshift

The fiscal challenges that began to build momentum in 2008 not only affected private-sector businesses, it also put a strain on government employers. Budget reductions and funding cuts meant that government employees did not have the same access to pay raises and performance bonuses they had in the past. The leadership of one government organization, the USDA, believed that employing a workplace strategy that embraced a distributed, off-site workforce would considerably reduce employee attrition during the type of protracted budget crunch created by the recent financial crisis. While the TEA of 2010 provided a mandate for agencies to develop telework opportunities for government employees, the USDA stands out among government employers as an agency that realized many unanticipated benefits from focusing on how to scale and leverage the program. As of February 2013, 75 percent of all USDA employees were eligible for telework, 48 percent have telework agreements, and 31 percent of the total eligible employee population is participating in telework.

The USDA's goal of increasing participation in telework over the last few years has resulted in significant expense reductions. Thousands of dollars are being saved in cost avoidance per employee, as USDA employees continue to participate in telework, even those who opt for one or two additional days per pay period. One example of this is through a transit subsidy program. Most recently, $2 million dollars of savings was achieved when the USDA executed its transit subsidy contract in fiscal year 2012.

This cost savings was directly attributed to the increased number of employees participating in telework.[3]

As we discussed earlier in this book, the USDA designed and deployed a telework strategy that originated with the goal of improving employee satisfaction and performance. The result has been a successfully deployed, formal telework and work-life flexibility program that is widely recognized as one that has engaged the workforce and fostered significant connection and commitment to the agency, a fact validated by the results of a survey report of US federal employees.[4]

Leveraging Workshift means to move beyond just realizing the immediate benefits of enabling flexible work and to successfully find ways to use those benefits to fundamentally add additional value to the organization and the population it serves. Up to this point, we have focused on how organizations have been successful in leveraging Workshift for the benefit of their own organizations. During our research, we learned of one organization that was leveraging Workshift to the benefit of other organizations.

In another example, Calgary, Alberta, Canada, a city of just over one million people, had seen a staggering growth rate of 26.5 percent over a ten-year period ending in 2012: an increase totaling approximately 223,000 new citizens. The city's transit and commuting infrastructure was heavily burdened by the need to support this population growth. Calgary, a natural resource-driven economy, and the energy resource capital of Canada, was facing a labor shortage. In 2009, companies competing for talent drove unemployment rates down to approximately 6.6 percent and downtown commercial real estate vacancy rates were hovering at only 6.9 percent.

Calgary Economic Development (CED), the city's lead economic development agency dedicated to attracting and retaining business investment and workforce, recognized an opportunity to position flexible/remote work as a strategy to not only reduce traffic congestion but support local organizations with the real estate challenges associated with a city burgeoning with population growth and to help Calgary companies attract and retain talent.

In 2009, the CED established a regional flexible work initiative program they branded WORKshift™, which sought to both raise awareness of remote work and support local organizations as they faced challenges of implementing flexible, mobility-friendly work places. From their perspective, supporting the local business community to accelerate the adoption of flexible work and successfully implement programs of their own was the way in which they could leverage value.

While Calgary was not the first city in North America to promote telework at the municipal level, the unusual approach and ultimate success of this particular program make it a model that is worth sharing and replicating. Their unique approach of having an economic development agency lead the regional provisioning of resources that support their business community is a powerful example of the results of leveraging program benefits, and we believe, a key trend of the future. With this approach, the team had an effective platform for uniquely positioning WORKshift™ as a solution to the challenges their community was facing from business-driven growth, rather than simply a commuter option to reduce gridlock, a model the team had seen deployed in other cities that they felt was limiting.

The results of the initiative were exciting and in the first few years of operations, the team reported in excess of 100 media hits, over 30 companies engaged, and a growing "normalization" and acceptance of remote work. In fact, a BMO commissioned poll from April 2013 shows a significant disparity in regional adoption of flexible work practices in Canada. Alberta led the country, with a 34 percent adoption rate, beating the national average by 11 percent! Perhaps most exciting, however, was an unanticipated benefit of the initiative including business attraction: the holy grail of economic development! Two companies selected Calgary as the base for their head office in Canada, attributing their decision partially to the existence of a Workshift-ready culture. This case demonstrates the very real economic opportunities associated with a leveraged opportunity at a macro community level.

The Value of Leverage

The common thread among the enterprises we've examined is that these organizations leveraged Workshift rather than just adopting it. Like most organizations, they started their programs much in the same way, with similar objectives as other programs, so their success in leveraging it did not occur because they had more resources, higher levels of commitment, or loftier goals. And it was not because they were in some specific, telework-friendly industry. The organizations we highlighted in this chapter are leaders in financial services, health care, call center, and the federal government—each uniquely different business sectors.

The difference, we found, was that organizations that successfully leveraged the value of their initiative did so by doing two things:

1. *Using results to generate more results*: Most organizations deploy new work arrangements, capture the benefits, and then stop there. Companies that realized the greatest value did so by aggressively using the results of creating a Workshift-enabled workplace to generate benefits in other areas of their business.
2. *Workshift as a differentiator*: Many companies benchmark their peers and try to emulate their competitors. Telework and flexible work arrangements are trendy; it's what organizations need to do to show they are keeping up with what everyone else is doing. However, for organizations, such as Alpine Access and CED, it was how they used the concept of remote working or telework to do something different, whether it was developing a new business model or helping to solve broader community challenges, which led to success and made it stand out.

For WellPoint, leveraging Workshift was clearly more of an acceptance management versus change management proposition than perhaps for any other company we interviewed. Conducting a due diligence exercise to assess the need to renew a lease was not new, but leveraging the company's OPW program as part of the decision-making criteria was. Although the program was already in place, heavily used, and yielding benefits to employees, it was not until their CRE leadership team tested assumptions that WellPoint realized significant benefits from understanding that increasing the cost efficiency of their operations meant delivering better value for their clients. For them, leveraging their existing OPW program to enable a dramatic reduction in real estate costs delivered value far beyond what was anticipated at their program's inception.

For the USDA, Workshift effectively differentiates the agency as an employer of choice among public and private organizations by offering a culture that fully takes the growth of flexible work options seriously and achieves consistent recognition for its telework initiative. Not only has this helped the USDA attract and retain employees, but also it has helped achieve agency cost efficiencies in areas previously unexpected.

The other common thread among the organizations mentioned in this chapter is that they didn't begin their programs with lofty goals of staggering benefits. Instead, each focused on developing a solid program and implementing it to meet specific needs of their organizations. It was this solid foundation that enabled each to be leveraged in ways that met needs to deliver significant and unexpected value to their organizations.

Leverage and the Future

In this chapter, we demonstrated how organizations leveraged their programs differently than others. While we found that an organization's ability to identify and realize opportunities is key to their program's success, we wonder if the future of Workshift, on a wider spectrum, perhaps even on a global scale, is contingent upon continuing to grow a list of positive business case studies. In our next chapter, we look at the growing trend of municipal entities adopting Workshift-friendly community strategies to meet multiple community-based goals. Community-driven programs are something Sheldon Dyck, president of ATB Investor Services believes is a compelling part of the future. In his words: The bigger story here is the possible impact of Workshift on communities, cities, countries and the globe. It could solve some of the biggest problems we face as a species. We are massive consumers of 'stuff' and now that there are so many of us we are producing a ton of undesirable byproducts from an environmental perspective. Start with just the possibility for a city. The biggest driver of dissatisfaction in cities is commute times. We react by spending billions of infrastructure dollars; most cities can't afford to move the same group of people at the same time of day from where they live to a central place to work. It is just absurd in terms of dollars and the impact on the quality of our lives. This does not need to be our reality any longer.

I think our firm and other leading companies have clearly demonstrated this. We have reduced our use of premises by 35 percent in one year and have taken the equivalent of a third of our workers off the road during rush hour. We did this while producing industry leading employee engagement scores, record levels of productivity, and receiving national awards for performance for our investors. Firms, cities, and regions that can master this change the fastest are going to have a massive competitive advantage, whether it's a firm competing for the best employees or a region competing for quality of life in an international labor market. This is the one 'arms race' that has few losers as the more places that make progress the greater the impact on our planet and the one ecosystem we all share.

Stage 7: Leverage—Summary

Key activities in this phase are:

- Promoting the program
- Ongoing communication, i.e., sharing the data, telling the story
- Tracking the results
- Identifying additional opportunities to capture benefits (financial and nonfinancial)

Deliverables:

- Implementation plan for broader organization
- Revised communication, training, and change acceptance plans
- Documented benefits (beyond initial program goals)

Key risks:

- Program stalling, fizzling out, or failing to expand
- Program is not linked to ongoing business strategy or performance management systems
- Results are not reviewed, or are reviewed inconsistently

CHAPTER 9

The Future of Workshift

> The fast moving trends get most of the attention. The slow moving trends have most of the power.
>
> —Stewart Brand, author of Whole Earth Catalog

Up to this point in our book, we have focused on the past and how a few organizations identified that their employees began to work differently, and illustrated ways in which those organizations responded to support those changes and leverage benefits of the new ways of working. In this chapter, we turn our attention to the future and the growing trend of Workshift by looking ahead. From our study of organizations that are expanding their acceptance of employees becoming more mobile and working more flexibly, we share examples of how cities are embracing it as a talent acquisition and economic development strategy, a way to augment civic innovation, and how some companies are developing new business models to keep up with the disruptive and dynamic changes in the market.

To successfully architect a strategic plan, one should begin with the future in mind. However, with the world and workplace now evolving at such an unprecedented pace, it's becoming increasingly difficult to successfully predict and plan for the future. In addition, while we struggle with our ability to predict how people will work, collaborate, and communicate years from now, we need to continue to identify and adapt to trends that surface today. In today's frenetic pace of innovation it's easy to find yourself comfortably surfing a trend wave today only to find you're under another tomorrow.

Thankfully, the rituals of a traditional work environment, which we have collectively accepted mostly without question—rush hour, cubicles, face-to-face meetings, and a lack of trust by managers—are becoming relics. Those who ignore signposts become extinct, and one striking example hails from Digital Equipment Corporation.

Digital, an American vendor of computing systems, at its peak in the late 1980s was one of the largest companies in the industry, second only to IBM. By the end of decade it was already rapidly declining. Why? Like many organizations, Digital failed to adapt to a rapidly changing marketplace. It ignored the markers urging transformative change and instead chose to rest on its history of success.

Ken Olsen, the founder and president of Digital, is infamously known for tragically declaring in 1977, "There is no reason for any individual to have a computer in his home."[1] Although some have pointed out that Olsen was actually referring to home automation and using computers to control all aspects of our personal lives, the quote has served as a reminder over the decades that even industry giants don't always predict the future well and risk their future by not recognizing trends quickly enough. Digital never adapted successfully after the personal computer eroded its minicomputer market, and in July 1992 the company's board forced Olsen to resign. The company was eventually broken up and sold for its parts, with Compaq acquiring much of the assets in 1998. But why is this important to the discussion on the changing workplace?

It's important because change happens quickly, and organizations and leaders who become mired in the past and resist evolution soon find themselves redundant, outdated, and irrelevant. Thinking ideas or organizations are invincible to change can be the kiss of death for many who hold on to outdated assumptions and methods of operation. The old assumption that companies are "too big to fail" simply isn't true in a world that has become increasingly biased toward organizations that are dexterous and nimble in approaching change and fostering creativity and innovation.

When thinking about the future, we collectively believe there are two compelling areas to consider as an organization constructs ways to integrate a broader vision for what it will become. These include: (1) the role of cities and government and how they will leverage Workshift to help solve multifaceted civic infrastructure/

urban development problems, and (2) the continued expansion of distributed companies that evolve flexible organizations into ones that fully bridge the gap between the traditional and the evolved workplace.

In this way, we can begin to imagine a possible future.

The Workshift-Enabled City

Throughout this book we have focused on how organizations, both public and private, have implemented programs for their own benefit and that of their employees. However, there is a new type of entity moving into the Workshift arena, and it is not an organization focused on realizing benefits for itself... at least not directly. Instead, it is driven toward identifying, enabling, and leveraging opportunities for a collection of many other organizations of different types, sizes, and business drivers. It is the Workshift-enabled city.

Like businesses, cities are facing unprecedented challenges. These include congestion, aging roads and public transit infrastructure, strained budgets, and an international and growing war for population and talent. To exacerbate things, in much of the Western world, productivity growth has slowly declined since the 1970s.

In some communities, these challenges are forcing community leaders to find new ways to innovate and to differentiate their cities in order to attract and retain the employers and businesses necessary to create jobs and fund or sustain operations. On the other end of the spectrum are cities with vibrant commercial ecosystems that are competing aggressively to attract the talent their business communities need to sustain industry growth. Whether the challenge is to bring in new businesses for economic development or to attract and retain new talent to sustain existing growth, forward thinking cities are beginning to discover the impact of embracing flexible work as a key component of their communities' overall fabric and infrastructure.

One example is a city we introduced in the previous chapter, Calgary, Alberta, Canada. WORKshift™ was established by CED as a promising and trusted brand in the Calgary marketplace in 2009 as local companies faced new challenges: a war for talent, increasing real estate costs, and longer commutes for their employees and citizens alike.

Seeking innovative solutions to common big city challenges, CED, the city's lead economic development agency dedicated to attracting and retaining business investment and workforce, recognized an opportunity to position flexible and remote work as a strategy to reduce congestion, to differentiate Calgary, and to support local organizations with real estate challenges associated with a city burgeoning with population and business growth.

The Canadian Federal Government had recently launched ecoMobility, a grant program dedicated to partnering with municipalities to create initiatives to reduce congestion and address greenhouse gas emissions and air pollution from transportation sources. CED, in partnership with the City of Calgary (that matched the grant by leveraging their own internal flexible work pilot program) secured funding to launch what started out as a three-year initiative to accelerate the adoption of flexible work practices in Calgary and the region. Key components of the multiyear plan for WORKshift™ Calgary included:

1. Engaging with key industry stakeholders to delineate an integrated strategy for the region;
2. Aligning with private and public partners to drive the development and deployment of the required regional programming;
3. Driving awareness and adoption in the business community;
4. Assessing the impacts of the integrated program on the community, organizations, and employees in the region;
5. Leveraging the Calgary regional telework initiative (branded WORKshift™ Calgary) to accelerate remote work adoption throughout the region, province, country, and globe; and
6. Creating a model that could be replicated in other jurisdictions.

WORKshift™ Calgary has been a pioneer in identifying and realizing ways to enable members of their business community to benefit from flexible work adoption. The program is unique in that it was led by an agency responsible for community economic development initiatives, rather than transportation, and targeted companies and corporate decision-makers rather than commuters or employees. Between 2009 and 2011, WORKshift™ leadership supported numerous organizations and thousands of employees, decision-makers, and commuters to help them assess the value of flexible work as it related to their key business and organizational challenges. As a result, the program successfully accelerated both the awareness and adoption of remote work in Calgary and has been recognized for its innovation and leadership both within Canada and beyond, with awards including:

- Royal Bank of Canada: "Most Innovative Economic Development Program"
- Landmark Projects designation
- Economic Development Achievement of the Year Award
- International Economic Development Council Gold award for sustainable and green initiatives
- Five international marketing awards

Throughout the life of the WORKshift™ initiative, CED focused on increasing awareness and education, leveraging new and existing relationships with the Canadian media, and exposing new data associated with the practice. In one instance they commissioned a report produced by Global Workplace Analytics, which found that Canadians with compatible jobs and a desire to work from home could have bottom-line impacts of over $53 billion per year for the country. Furthermore, the study reported that enabling these employees to participate in WORKshift™ would generate energy and environmental benefits that would include a reduction in greenhouse gas emissions equivalent to taking a third of Montreal solo-drivers out of the commute and realize an annual savings of 389 million liters of gasoline (see table 9.1).

As a result of the successes in Calgary, WORKshift™ became increasingly recognized and associated with the transformation of

Table 9.1 Annual bottom-line benefits

Participants	*1*	*250*	*Canada (millions)*
Employer	$10,037	$2,492,146	$44,000
Employee	$1,939	$484,738	$8,500
Community	$132	$32,940	$578
Overall	$12,108	$3,009,825	$53,100

Source: Global Workplace Analytics, The Bottom Line Benefits of Workshifting.

the work experience. This transformation, enabling more workers to experience flexible work arrangements, increases their productivity, improves corporate loyalty, and reduces environmental impacts of the corporation and within the urban environment. It not only gained traction in the Calgary marketplace, but has also sparked a surge of interest from a number of cities in Canada and beyond that have sought support from CED in establishing their own programs.

WORKshift™ created a successful brand promise and unique municipal approach that has the potential to be adopted by major cities around the globe. We believe it has the capacity to change the landscape of the way we live, work, and play, and can address some of the principal challenges we are facing and will continue to face with a growing global population and increased urbanization. It is a case study that demonstrates that through partnerships with industry and various levels of government, transformation can be achieved, with benefits being realized by businesses and citizens alike.

Transportation Demand Management

In addition to embracing Workshift as a valuable tool to support commerce in their communities, cities are beginning to identify remote work as being instrumental in strategic transportation demand management (TDM). TDM is a strategy designed to inform people about available travel options and to encourage improvements in how and when to travel. The objective is to get fewer people driving alone during the peak period to ease congestion.

Flexible work options, like flextime and compressed work weeks, play a significant role in supporting TDM goals. They allow employees to coordinate work schedules with personal commitments and adjust when they travel, with the community benefitting from the reduction of traffic congestion. Flexible work schedules reward employees with time saved from eliminated trips on remote workdays and compressed work week days off. These strategies coupled with technology also enable some workers to avoid peak travel times by starting their workday at home addressing emails, then traveling off-peak to the office to complete their workday.

Organizations that have embraced flexible work schedules are supporting the reduction of traffic congestion in major metropolitan areas by easing commuting for employees. Lisa Lyssand, VP of HR and facilities with BroadVision, stated that the company's mobile work style is led from the top down. "We employ adults, we expect them to do their jobs where they are and when they need to be in a place together, they come together." With such flexible work schedules, BroadVision employees, based in northern California, know they are able to save an inordinate amount of time bypassing the several hours it can take to get anywhere in the San Francisco Bay Area during peak commute hours, and are helping to reduce carbon emissions along the way.

"People who choose alternatives to driving alone during peak period traffic become part of the traffic congestion solution," Ron Schafer, TDM specialist for City Calgary told us. "Our transportation systems have capacity to move many people, just not all at the same time. Anything that we can do individually to reduce the number of vehicles on the road during peak periods will make the journey more pleasant for all of us." As the saying goes, "You're not in traffic, you are the traffic!"

TDM groups have a mandate to reduce pressure on roads and transit. Of particular interest to these groups is reducing peak pressures during rush hour and peak times. Previous tactics have included promoting carpooling, and active transportation such as cycling and walking. The trouble with these strategies is that only a small percent of the population would consider this behavioral change. By cities supporting and promoting adoption they are able to leverage a transportation demand strategy that is attractive to many segments of the employee population, which offers one of the most effective modes of reducing pressure on infrastructure. While cycling and active transportation in places like Copenhagen and Amsterdam represent a state of utopia for many TDM planners, it seems an unlikely outcome in our cities given the state of modal choices in North America today. For immediate and significant change we will need to meet people where they are, and many can already work from home—with high-speed internet access just waiting to be given permission to avoid unnecessary commutes. If only many more employers would just understand the opportunity!

Commuting time is, more often than not, lost time. One does not generate value or increase wellness sitting in traffic. It is time not being spent reading more, enjoying family time, participating in a hobby, or realizing other wellness pursuits—or even working! According to Stats Data, the average business person in Toronto spends 79 minutes every day just getting to and from work. This means the equivalent of approximately 40 eight-hour working days of personal and professional productivity are lost. Eliminating just one of those commutes a week would return 64 hours of time per year per person.

We believe these types of community-led initiatives are a key component of the next phase of Workshift growth. Cities must become more willing to embrace such initiatives, measure the impacts, and leverage the benefits in their community, and municipal leaders need to learn to prioritize this as a key strategy to differentiate their cities and attract the resources necessary for sustainable growth. For example, imagine the impact of having the data to demonstrate that a community-based Workshift program could reduce citizen commuting by even 5 percent, resulting in a reduction of 1,000,0000 miles driven annually as well as the corresponding elimination of CO^2 emissions? How would that affect the overall challenges with congestion in your city? What kinds of new and innovative thinking and business would crop up? What would it be worth?

Workshift is an important space for cities to embrace, as it involves the convergence of environmental sustainability, business profitability, employee engagement and work-life integration, municipal functionality, and technology, which is becoming a priority for municipalities.

A Purely Distributed Company Model

While many companies realize success through a deliberate focus on strategy, planning, and execution, others have gone much farther to create successful organizations based entirely on the concept of a purely distributed model. Some organizations have difficulty envisioning how they could ever become entirely distributed, but one company we introduced in chapter 4, Automattic, a leading web publishing/software platform for web development, provides an excellent example of what this model can look like, which we believe may become more commonplace in the future. While you consider Automattic, ask yourself: Do you think you or your company could, or would like to, work in this fashion? Do you think it will be the norm for companies of the future to work in this construct?

Toni Schneider, CEO of Automattic, shared that the company has experienced strong growth and has done so by being a uniquely distributed company, right from its origins to present day. Workshift for Automattic is so ingrained in their culture, that Toni shared, "For us, working this way is second nature. We think it's not that big of deal to have this freedom and flexibility, it seems kind of normal. But, I've talked to other CEOs who are blown away, wondering how do we do this? We have 160+ employees and we are adding one to two new employees per week."

On the business of being a distributed company, Toni further added that, "A software company is perfect for this kind of distributed model. Engineers need peace and quiet and no interruptions to write software. We have open source projects that are a perfect example of how this kind of collaboration is going on. Thousands of people are contributing, nothing is centralized, we have very little formality and rules of how people contribute which is part of our culture."

While this way of working may seem unrealistic to some, many aspects of what works in this distributed model underscores how important transparency is and how it can solve a lot of problems. To let people know what's going on, Automattic employees use internal blogs daily so everyone sees what everyone is talking about, which breeds a more open culture. This transparency starts from the top and permeates to each employee. Other than personal HR issues, investor meetings, business meetings, notes, board packages, and financials, for example, are all shared. To do it this way helps reduce overhead and provides employees a sense of being in the know.

In addition to transparency, a distributed environment requires that you be self-directed, Toni added. "When you make your own decisions, there is less of an ability to constantly check in and stay on top of things. You have to move away from the top down model and understand, how do I support people and let them figure out what do to? This changes the nature of management, puts the individual more in charge and on top of their own world and how they get things done in their job. The company then puts services around them to support how they work. These supports empower everyone individually vs. the older model less distributed companies are known for: you are coming here, here are the rules, fit yourself in here. Automattic is less focused on making people do things in a certain way because at the end of the day is it about getting things done and results and I really don't care how it gets done."

In a purely distributed company, managers are more important than ever. Managers need to know what kinds of skills are needed to be effective. Just because you're distributed, it doesn't mean the planning, oversight, and coordination aspects of management go away. There is an opportunity for traditional managers to learn the following: You still need to plan and communicate and this distributed way of working is an opportunity to work more efficiently and is the way employees want to work today.

On the unanticipated benefits of having leveraged this company model, Toni added: We set out to democratize online publishing, and being a successful distributed company is a byproduct of how we went about this. We are the first few people who happened to be distributed in open source and thought, let's keep going. We said we'll try it but it wasn't a huge goal. I am surprised at how being a distributed company is so central to our culture. We've had a lot of success with WordPress and the way we've built our organization is getting as much attention as the product itself. It's a surprise—we sometimes think we're contributing to help making distributed organizations work is as much of what we do in building WordPress. How broadly that has resonated is very satisfying. Because of how well it's worked for us, people assume how/why it's grown so quickly; some competitors assume how/why we are growing. The distributed piece has been so important to us and successful for us, I'm glad people are learning about it. If I had to guess, the reason why it's getting more press is because the business is doing so well. Big open source projects were operating this way 20 years ago, but businesses would look at it and say, this only works in a volunteer loosely collaborating fashion. When you add success to the equation and competitive advantage, people take note.

Toni further shared: "We are working in a distributed model as a business and not a different type of organization. More people are paying attention and that's noticeable. For those with open source or engineering backgrounds—it feels like we've been operating this way forever—but the new piece is that it's a high growth business. To me the next set of challenges is how do you make this work in other businesses? The interesting question is, if and how do these ideas apply to more traditional companies and how far can it go? Some businesses, it may not be possible to be purely distributed, but I wouldn't be surprised if in 10–20 years it will be much more broadly in use than it is today."

Conclusion

Whether it's just one part of an overall workplace strategy, such as with Trend Micro, BCBSMA, or the USDA, or the only way an organization works, like at Automattic or Alpine Access, there is little doubt that the Workshift trend is growing. However, after studying many organizations for this book, we were curious as to why the pace of adoption varied so greatly from business to business. We asked Sheldon Dyck, president of ATB Investor Services, about his thoughts on this phenomenon, and he suggested the pace of Workshift adoption is not atypical when compared to other transformational changes in business. In time, the pace of Workshift adoption will improve exponentially, but because many leaders lived through or saw the failure of the early adopters they remain complacent that it won't work. They hold this belief even though the reasons it failed at first have long since been solved. The telework era, the first wave of the Internet, and early cell phones all went through similar phases. You will always have a group of leaders who say, "Yeah, I've tried this before and it doesn't really work that well." Or, "This is a nice perk, but it couldn't possibly work in our organization."

Sheldon identified complacency as a barrier to adoption, so we wondered if it was really a failure of early stage attempts to implement programs as some surmise or really, as he stated, something more akin to inertia. Sheldon elaborated, "It's only been in the past seven to eight years where the rules have completely changed and the enabling technologies matured allowing high quality virtual commuting and collaboration. Not surprisingly, our leadership styles rooted in 300 years of managing factory workers haven't yet shifted. There were also a few decades of world wars in that time that engrained command and control management into generations of leaders. It's understandable given our past that the vast majority of leaders aren't unleashing the power of Workshift. In typical fashion the first iteration of remote working didn't help the cause. Laptops and cell phones are nice tools, but sending someone home to work using only those resources completely ignored the fact that humans are social animals and people need to get more from work than just a pay check."

But what about the next iteration? Sheldon observed that, "We're going through a typical 'dark ages' period where the possibility to work in a more productive and rewarding way is not being widely embraced. The reality is that we'll be leading organizations that look completely different tomorrow than they do today because they are going to be virtual or distributed organizations—not physical ones. You may think you have a hall pass because you still make products and that this only applies to service organizations and professional firms, but I think you are kidding yourself if you cling to that ideal. With manufacturing now on the cusp of having that kind of capability via 3D printing and other technologies, it's not long before they are deeply affected as well."

Based on his success leading a Workshift-enabled organization, we asked Sheldon if he had any advice for the leaders of organizations struggling to move to this next iteration of the workplace. "For an organization to make this shift it has to be modelled and championed by the people at the top, first and foremost the CEO. That shouldn't be a surprise as that is the key to making any transformative shift a reality. For leaders that are struggling with this change, I would encourage them to think about these questions: Where do you think the best talent in the world is going to work? Do you think the best people are going to choose companies like ours where people can have the best possible personal life, create the best possible career results, and feel good about the impact they are having on their community, or do you think they are going to work for companies that force them to have a two hour commute every day? Do you want to limit your talent pool to people who can and are willing to drive to your physical locations or do you want a talent pool that is the best of the 7 billion people on the planet? Which side of that equation do you want to be on?"

Throughout this book we have examined various organizations that are all evolving in numerous ways. The terms we often use to describe these changes, whether they are telecommuting, teleworking, or flexible work practices, seem to come and go like many management fads. Regardless of the taxonomy, there is no denying that the workplace is irrevocably changing. In the very near future, working in an assigned office cubicle that is co-located with all other employees for set hours every day may seem as old fashioned or outdated as working with typewriters or punch cards. Whether organizations make dramatic 180-degree turns or lead a quiet revolution that seamlessly acclimates to using new technology remains to be seen. Change is the only constant, and organizations must be willing to adapt or risk their future.

Still, resistance to new ways of working will persist in many organizations. The physics of the office place have always been present. Changes in employee interactions, introduction of new technology, and altering work schedules or habits are bound to create reactions or objections. As PopTech Executive Director Andrew Zolli has said, "Humans are notoriously bad at anticipating events that don't conform to a very narrow idea of what the future will be which is why we're often caught off guard by the unexpected." We believe that the leaders and organizations that best prepare their employees for the future, like the many companies and agencies we spoke with, will be those that are more open, flexible, and willing to accept new ideas invading the workplace.

Will we all work from home full time in some futuristic manner, with holograms and flying cars? Perhaps, but it's hard to know whether this will occur in our lifetimes. We do know, however, that organizations that fully embrace more mobile work styles and follow a path to embed them into corporate cultures while evolving the role of managers are proving their competitive advantage. And the normalization of a highly mobile, technologically savvy workforce motivated by meaning and working in a team-focused project construct is a very likely future state for most organizations and cities. With disruptive business changes happening fast, organizations have to remain vigilant to present-day realities that can make future thinking a distant but necessary priority.

Remember, the future sneaks up on you.

Notes

Introduction: The Evolved Workplace

1. Partnership for Public Service and Booz Allen Hamilton, *On Demand Government: Deploying Flexibilities to Ensure Service Continuity* (Washington, DC, 2010).
2. Mineta Transportation Institute, *Facilitating Telecommuting: Exploring the Role of Telecommuting Intensity and Differences between Telecommuters and Non-Telecommuters* (San Jose, CA, 2010).

2 Investigate

1. Metcalf, Fran, "Working With, Not For, The Boss," *Career Advice*,. http://career-advice.careerone.com.au/career-development/profcssional-development/working-with-not-for-boss/article.aspx

3 Discover

1. Levinson, Meredith, "Business Strategy: The 'Best Determinant' for Project Success," *CIO* (November 7, 2009), http://www.cio.com/article/508018; Project Management Institute, *Linking Project Management with Business Strategy* (Seattle, Washington, DC, 2006).
2. Mineta Transportation Institute, *Facilitating Telecommuting: Exploring the Role of Telecommuting Intensity and Differences between Telecommuters and Non-Telecommuters* (San Jose, CA, 2010).
3. Betts, Mitch, ed., *BYOD: The Bring-Your-Own-Device Phenomenon* (Framingham, MA: CXO Media, 2012), 4.
4. US Green Building Council, "LEED 2009 for Existing Buildings Operations and Maintenance" (Washington, DC, 2009.)

4 Design

1. "Leveraging Mobility, Managing Plan: How Changing Work Styles Impact Real Estate and Carbon Footprint," GSA Public Buildings Service, 2010.
2. "What Really Works: Lessons Learned from 25 Years of Workplace Flexibility," *Working Mother Magazine*, IBM, 2010.
3. Dr. Michael O'Neill and Tracy Wymer, "The Metrics of Distributed Work: Financial and Performance Benefits of an Emerging Work Model," Knoll Workplace Research, 2011.
4. Schneider, Toni, "Five Reasons Why Your Company Should Be Distributed," www.toni.org, March 2010.
5. Charles Grantham and Jim Ware, "Flexible Work Arrangements for Non Exempt Employees," *World At Work*, SR-02–09, 2009.
6. Ibid.
7. Jennifer Swanberg and Liz Watson, "Flexible Workplace Solutions for Low-Wage Hourly Workers: A Framework for a National Conversation," Workplace Flexibility 2010 and The Institute for Workplace Innovation, 2010.
8. Anacona, Deborah, "Leadership in an Age of Uncertainty," MIT Leadership Center, 2005.
9. Kim Elsbach, Dan Cable, and Jeffrey Sherman, "How Passive 'Face Time' Affects Perceptions of Employees: Evidence of Spontaneous Trait Inference," *Human Relations* 63, no. 6 (June 2010): 735–760.

5 Engage

1. Kotter, John, *Leading Change* (Boston: Harvard Review Press, 1996).
2. Several recent independent studies of both public- and private-sector organizations all indicate that the biggest, or at least one of the biggest, challenge to implementing telework programs is management resistance, including:Mineta Transportation Institute, *Facilitating Telecommuting: Exploring the Role of Telecommuting Intensity and Differences between Telecommuters and Non-Telecommuters* (San Jose, Ca, 2010).United States Office of Personnel Management, *Status of Telework in the Federal Government: Report to Congress* (Washington, DC, 2011), 15–16.Partnership for Public Service and Booz Allen Hamilton, *On Demand Government: Deploying Flexibilities to Ensure Service Continuity* (Washington, DC, 2010).US Merit Systems Protection Board, *Telework: Weighing the Information, Determining an Appropriate Approach* (Washington, DC, 2011), 34.

3. LaClair, Jennifer A., and Ravi P. Rao, "Helping Employees Embrace Change," *McKinsey Quarterly* (November 2002), https://www.mckinseyquarterly.com/Helping_employees_embrace_change_1225
4. McKinsey & Company, *McKinsey Global Survey Results: What Successful Transformations Share* (Chicago, 2010).
5. Martin, B. H., "Has Telework Been Framed? The Influence of Framing Effects on the Telework Adoption Decision in Organizations," Doctoral dissertation, University of Calgary (Canada), 2012, ProQuest, UMI Dissertations Publishing, NR87917.
6. Ibid. p 1.
7. Ibid. pp. 97–98.
8. Ibid. p. 1.

8 Leverage

1. Implementing Integrated Work, KNOLL Research, KNOLL, Oct 2010, http://www.knoll.com/knollnewsdetail/implementing-integrated-work
2. "Evolution of the Networked Enterprise," McKinsey Global Survey, March 2013.
3. NARFE Magazine, May 2013, http://issuu.com/narfe/docs/narfe052013.
4. "2012 Status of Telework in the Federal Government," United States Office of Personnel, June 2012.

9 The Future of Workshift

1. Edgar H. Schein, Paul J Kampas, Peter S Delisi, and Michael M. Sonduck, *DEC Is Dead, Long Live DEC* (San Francisco: Berrett-Koehler, 2003), 38–40.

Index